Other Books by Paulette G. Cohen

The Love in Life Listening, With Over 100 Poetry of inspiration.
(2001) 1st book Library

A Guide on Spiritual Growth. (2002) 1st book Library

It's Just a Matter of Respect!! (2004) AuthorHouse

This Is Dedicated to the Ones I Love and the Ones I Thought Loved Me!

Sultry and Very Sensual Poems for That Special You. Spoken on the Real Tip from This Woman's Lip!

Paulette G. Cohen "inspiration"

authorHOUSE

AuthorHouse™
1663 Liberty Drive
Bloomington, IN 47403
www.authorhouse.com
Phone: 1 (800) 839-8640

Published by AuthorHouse 12/30/2016

ISBN: 978-1-5246-5730-7 (sc)
ISBN: 978-1-5246-5729-1 (e)

Library of Congress Control Number: 2016921438

Print information available on the last page.

Any people depicted in stock imagery provided by Thinkstock are models, and such images are being used for illustrative purposes only.
Certain stock imagery © Thinkstock.

This book is printed on acid-free paper.

`You I acknowledge & Dedicate!

This book was written for very special people in my life. First, I would like to thank my Heavenly mother/father God and Lord Jesus Christ, for loving me as He does and giving me this incredible strength to be able to move forward in my life with such a positive way that I ever imagined. The spirit of love and peace has entered my soul and given me the order of good to put forward what is best for me. I thank the man above for lifting me so that I may see my life a little clearer. Thank you so much God! It is He who holds the reason behind it. Dig carefully into each part and listen to the message. The truth about love is <u>You</u> are wonderful!

Second, I would like to say, when I wrote this book there was someone I truly loved in my life. There also were certain friends I had who held a special place in my heart. However, they wound up breaking it, before this book was published. All I can say is this: I dedicate the many poems to you, from when you made me happy, all the way until you made me sad. I hope you see through my pain with the power of poetry and how you made me feel during those times.

Without another word to say, my children to whom I bore, I dedicate all of me to you, I am so proud of you!

To my two Aunt whom I love so much, Mrs. Rosa McArthur Thank you for sticking by my side.

Finally as always but never the least, my great and wonderful Spirit within. Thank you for showing me the ways once again. I could not have made the choices that I have if you did not point the directions. Thank you God in me!

Faith is so important in my life that I advise everyone to

look into your soul and thank the Holy man himself for giving you the ways to live! What you may think is not important is very important! What you may think is important, is not!

We all have to believe in ourselves <u>first, and then</u> we will understand the many happenings that we encounter.

God is Good! All the time!

The Introduction!

This book of love poems and not so loving poems is different from the ones I have done before, because it is dedicated to God and the many people who played a part in my life growing up! A chip off my novel: It's Just a Matter of Respect! This book express how I feel about some of the people I mentioned in my earlier books.

I have this urge to tell the world how I feel. I think when you meet a person who motivates you in a strong direction, becomes a reason to talk about. However way you do it does not matter. I choose to express myself through the power of poetry. That's who I am, a woman of God, poet and a woman of many different areas in this portion of living. I have listened to my heart, soul, mind, and body throughout this journey I am on called life. I have met many people and seen many things. When coming upon a blessing full of people, I want to write about them.

I do dedicate this book to the one's I love, and the one's I thought loved me. That covers a small percent, but the people involved is all that matters. You know who you are and how we met. I had to seek a thousand times into what God has given me to find you. The treasure that is buried beneath the wind of my soul is very delicate, but the strength that I have been blessed to endure has made me most knowledgeable about what is going on in my life.

I am inviting all of you into the many sections of the real world of love, and misunderstood!   MY WORLD! Each part is just as important as the other. I am dividing certain issues because it applies to particular people understanding what we feel from ourselves and allowing another to receive it. Love in an expanding way of sensualness. The pure caressing of the human mind and body, and the sexual intensity of knowing. Knowing how to love, knowing when to love, and knowing how to receive it without being a little under whelmed!

I know what lies beneath my every whim of this journey I have been blessed to enter, but there is so much more to learn. Everyday I take the golden opportunity to thank myself for accepting who I am and will be. God is love, and he made me to be one in a million. My expressions are sincere to those involved. So, as I continue with all said, I will be who I am, "inspiration"

And without further delay, let me open the doors to a little motivation from our source of Love from above God himself. It is He who gave me the power and the strength to remain calm throughout the many challenges I faced while writing this book. As you can see, the result is over exciting to share with all of you. I am breathing again. Let me step up to the plate, for yet another earth shattering event is about to begin. Come with Me!

Table of Contents

Part Two Of This Journey!

Part Three Of This Journey!

Part Four Of This Journey!

Part Five Of This Journey!

Part Six Of This Journey!

Part Seven Of This Journey!

Part Eight Of This Journey!

Part One Of This Journey!

This is the beginning of my magnificent journey into this thing we call love! Love, oh how sweet the taste is when coming out of your mouth. This is the genuine side of me. Very sultry, soft, sexy, and loving poems that will make him melt. Say it to him at anytime. You know there is no right or wrong time for you to tell someone that you love him or her. The right time is now, because I know some of you are waiting for that special moment. Is there really a special moment? I say NO! At this time we all need to hear it from someone. Well let me start by saying; I love all of you. If I did not, it would be hard for me to express myself the way I do.

Live out this section and exercise some of the deep emotional ways to speak. It's aright! There is no wrong or right way to say it, just do it!

Are you ready for me? Hold on, because this one is better than the first. Did you read The Love in Life Listening with Over 100 Soulful Poetry of "inspiration"? If you did, then take an even deeper breath, because I am about to knock your socks off, so HOLD ON! Enjoy the many parts of love in this section with over 40 personal poems dedicated to the one's I love!

This I Promise You!

Although time has passed, and we
Both have moved on,
A part of me is playing a certain song.

It lives inside me from now until
             Whenever,
I guess when we finally can be
             Together

If I said it once, I will say it again,
I'm open to receive your love, until
             The end.

We both have faced so many challenges not so good.
But me & you as we, was not one
             Of those that stood!

I know we both have had some pain,
But this I promise you I'll never shame!

While you are away from me these
             next few weeks,
My kisses are waiting to land on your cheeks.

I want you to know what you mean to me,
This I promise you because my soul is free!
Free to hold you, free to love with all
             that I am

This I promise you, not some phony
                Scam
There will always be something special to remember.
Like the night we met 2002 September!

Take this with you while you are away,
This I promise you more than words
                Will ever say.

You are the one that makes me smile.
I hope it is not to late to make
Our love worth more than a while!

Let Me Kiss You For A Change

It's easy for me to accept who I am.
It's even easier to know what I want.
And standing up for what I believe
        Is what I do!

My heart is strong, my soul is even better.   But my needs have not been met.

When I hold you and look in your eyes, there's a secret that hides the truth.

Your pain = my pain, because of a small connection.

Are you pampered today?
How about your ego, have it been
                Stroked?

Tell me something, how many female
Frogs have you kissed?

How many princesses have kissed you
                Back?

Let me kiss you for a change!
Feel the difference of my lips.

Let me blow succulent truth
throughout your ears. My truth!

Somewhere deep inside, you feel
The hora and appreciate it.

Well here's mines!
Let me kiss you for a change!
And I guarantee you, will feel
The difference!

<u>A Different You</u>

Your voice peaked
     My interest
The very first time
I spoke with you!

Amazingly enough I felt a
        Soothing Spirit
When I first talked to you.

There was a difference!
        I knew it so
I smiled.

Then I saw you
       And broadened my
Cheek bones.
       Tall, very studious,
With a chest structure so neat.

          Your waist is long
But as I see you walking
          I understood how
Well you carry YOU!

        What you shared with
Me
     Made my day!
What you said to me made my
        Afternoon!
   What you did to me,
Made my night!

Sometime ago
I asked God
                    About you!

And I did not even know
                    Who
You
                    Were!

But he did!
                    There's a different
Type of you,

Which leave a pleasant taste
                    In
My
                              Mouth!
And I love the way it feels.
Don't
          Change
                    What
                         You
                              Have
                                   Brought
To this Universe!

     Because we don't need another,

Just the same as the others!

48 Hours With You!

About 3 weeks ago you told me
You wanted to take me away.
Needless to be, I had nothing
to say.

As time went by you gave me
the date.

I was happy to know that I would
be spending time with my soul mate.
As the days came near and the nights
made me smile,
I figured that at least for two days
your number I would not have to dial.

So then it came that wonderful time,
that I could spend with you ringing
more than your chime.

I watched you drive the wheel so
Good.
I admired how you stood as a man
should!

You took the role and played it well.
No kind of Bull---- you were trying
to sell.
When we arrived safe and sound,
the only thing I could hear was
my heart about to pound.

Because you are so fine, not quite

9

all mines, but what I have to share
Is more than any man but you could
bare.

So, what we did that night was great.
I got to gaze in your eye like a first
date.

The love we shared is in full bloom.
My moans and your groans filled
the entire room.

As I awoke to see your beautiful face.
I felt so lucky and in love because
I have good taste.

Saturday was filled with more than a
dream.
It felt very alive not what it seemed.

Being with you made me see!
48 hours with you is not enough for
me!

<u>Magic</u>

Today I looked into my soul just to see
all the conversations we shared together.
       To my surprise I listened to a mysterious sound that entered
the womb of my heart.
       It was the echo of your sweet and most talented voice. Then
I heard you say shhh! So I kept quite.
Now as I think back at all those wonderful times
       that I just sat down and mesmerized the moment
       by momentsteps when there was no other like you
       in my life, I could not believe how all of a sudden
       the magic came into a form of the man that stood
       there right before my eyes. You!
       Love me forever as I will be your slave to the
rhythm of our joy! You came into my life like
       the brisk of the breeze that makes the flowers
grow tall and stimulating. The body of the water
       that falls from Niagara down the stream of the river in my
heart. Oh I know I love you. I know what blood line of happiness
has come about my body of motion. Oh I need you! I need your
sweet cake and rock candy between those wonderful two body parts
that help you stand tall.
       Yes my dear lovely one, you are magic
I know this because when I am near you, all the
       ugly emotion disappears! And you appear
with your dynamic sense of sensations that make
       my mouth pucker and my lips wet.
Mr. Magic keep singing the music
       the way you do. Strum my drum anytime.
              Thank you!
for being the you God blessed you to be.

An Apple Green Mood

One afternoon towards the evening I thought about you!
       After a shower, bath, and splash of
perfume or two.
       I gazed in the mirror and said, "Damn
I look good"
       Nice big butt formed the way it should!
I smiled then winked, at what I saw,
       Because once upon a time there was
sadness and a sunken jaw.
       Today is a new day and I feel fresh and
clean.
       I am so delighted and filled with gleam!
A lime green bra with thongs to match,
       If you saw what I did, you'd want to be
attached!
       It was you who put me in this direction.
Thinking about just the way you stood with an erection!
       I placed my thongs straight up my tush,
not caring how little it covered my bush!
       My breast were sitting straight up and
high,
       When you see me, you'll lick them like a
banana cream pie!
       I'm in an apple green mood for sure!
What can I say? If you see them, your lips can take a tour!
       So please be gentle while approaching me,
I am so bright and lovely but not for everyone to see.
       As I stroll around the room so smooth &
slow, You can devour me from head to toe!

12

Not just apple green or even hot pink!
No matter what I wear, I'll make you think.
It's nice to be nice in all that you do,
May take a while, but its worth more than a few.
I'm in an apple green mood as I observe just who I am,
Not being cocky, but loving what God has put in demand!

Your Music Speaks To Me!

At Midnight I turn you on
to get turned on by you.
       The music starts coming up
loud and clear. As I open up my mind
       to understand what is going on
and what is being said. I truly love
       your language.
The language of smooth lust.
       Your music speaks to me.
The words, the mix, the harmony,
       sweet, sweet, sensible and delightful.
so mellow and grooving to the inner
       experience.
Your jewel, your fingertips stroking the
       vinyl that plays!
I watched the radio as I heard and smelled
       the sound of you cumming through
the speakers.
       Your music speaks to me.
nice and loud as you move back and forth
       from fast to slow to soulful
over that Jazz that soaks me up!
       Oh, you know what to do, so gifted
so talented, and very sexy.
       Just the way it should sound.
Sensuous and confidant very alluring.
       Your music speaks to me.
Well I hear you. So, keep playing
       Those songs that make my body curl. And booty swirl!

The Love Of My Life

You are my love, my source, my creator,
Every thing a woman should want.
You have proved that I am capable of passion.
Passion that goes beyond the norm, passion
That forms into a whole which bonds to the
Other side.
You have motivated me in so many directions
I would ever have imagined, and the love,
Oh it's amazing when I wake up each morning
Just knowing, and feeling the presence of you
Near.
Now I smile- my teeth are full of whiteness so
I grin. Then I stare up to the sky feeling you
Plant the warmness of a kiss to my soul.
You are the love of my life- my inspiration
And all there is to know about man, woman or
Child.
What will you show me today? My heart is
Open to learn as, my Spirit lingers on to
Suggestions that I may follow.
As I get up and is welcomed by you, all I see
Is my face, because you have placed another
Blessing upon me. That is myself!

Lonely

When you are there but I cannot reach you, trying to receive your affection, but losing my mind. I think I hear you but when I looked around my body shook. Was it you or my imagination? Why is it that we as women really miss a man so much but, for him it's, well I'm ok. The heart is so fragile and gentle; I wonder if he realizes he makes it hurt.

When a woman doesn't see the man she loves, doesn't hear from the man she loves, doesn't taste the man she loves, for a period of time, she gets lonely.

I don't want to be alone again. I don't want to be away from you. I don't want to lose you, because, there is no one that can fill me like you. Your emotions, your ways, your smile, and your love is all it takes so, wherever you are, whatever it takes, come to me and take the pain away.

I don't want to be lonely anymore!

Not So Ordinary

The type of man who is always talking with a
tone of softness.
A little less than 6'0 with a rock hard structure that
made me raise my eyebrow.
The illusion if I ever had one would be too simply
run my desire from within.
In a mountain so high, not only would I take you
with me but, I would never
deny you to enter my womanhood-
Shaven head with the most kissable lip
structure.
The eyes although hidden a tinge bit with
the mystery of darkness has a strong secret within.
You always smile but, on the inside
I'm sure you have this extraordinary grin. -
And that butt, ohh, ohh! So round and
tastily touchable.
Every time I see it, I want to hold it in the
Palm of my hands.
Your legs are use to being in motion,
I can tell by the way they move.
Your hands are very swift in action
Because you use them wisely.
Your chest makes me curl just
To feel it.
All this together makes a not so ordinary
Person. -
Your taste glorifies me whenever I look up
at this universe- no one is like you- no one can replace you-
you're my dream come true.
That is why you are not so ordinary!

It's So Special

One night I decided to get into your
                 Almond delight!
When you telephoned me I had such a
                 Big and broad awakening
On my face- feel what I am about to say.
                 The cologne you wear is so amazing to
My nose.
                 And as I sniff at your mental affection
I realize how much you care.
                 When you hold me front, back, to the
Side I just lay back and think about all that is,
                 All that could be, and all that was.
You are special! You know why? Because you
                 Got me! Oh yea our sex, our love, our
Pleasure, our undivided togetherness is so good,
          So detectable, so sweet. Do you feel me?
It's all that! It's so special, that I want to reach
          Beneath the nines and tens of every
Roman numerical that we would ever imagine.
          So special that when you stroll around with
That sort of seriousness makes all eyes
          Turn to your attention. So special that
Although I am as magnified as you are fine,
          Our vibratory level meets before we are
Near each other.
                 You are that Special!

Why Can't We Communicate?

There are so many ways to get a point across.
Why can't we communicate?
The telephone line is open 24-7
Why can't we communicate?
I live near you not in another city
Come by me sometimes and say hello.
Why can't we communicate?
A letter is nice once in a while.
Why can't we communicate?
Communication is so important to the soul
It relaxes you. Helps to make those inner
Points relieved, less stress on the mind.
Just say what you want and don't be afraid
To talk to me.
I will listen if you are there.
That's what communication is!

<u>I Just Want To Say Thank You</u>

Thank you for entering my life, letting me know
There are still good people out here.
Thank you for being such a man to this woman
Standing in front of you.
Thank you for bearing your heart to me.
Thank you for letting more people see that a black
Man can be exceptionally intelligent.
Thank you for your spirit uniting with mines.
Thank you for all the wonderful messages that
God sends to you and what you share with me.
You see, I have experienced being around many
Different people and they are so negative.
But your positive affect moves me!
Your enlightment, which makes me smile, is
So wonderful!
I know I can count on you when I need some joyous
Words.
You are very moving and I just want to say Thank you!

Devotion

There was a time that I couldn't even
Be stable to stay with someone.
        My trust in my world had shattered.
Then, I threw the towel in.
        Thinking about the wonderful woman
I am and how devoted I would be with the right man.
        Now being as grown up and flossy as I am
Devoted to reaching for a higher statue in life that
        May be far fetched for others, but not me!
Yes I am the devoted one.
        The one that has stood her strong grounds and
Showed her capabilities to another length that even
        You wouldn't expect.
I am devoted to making this life here work.
        Devoted to following my dreams to the path it
Leads, and whosoever should come before me,
        I am devoted to you in making us we and
Continuing our lives of darkness to ever shine.
        I am devoted, I am a queen of love, so whenever
Your ready- don't ever hesitate to come before me.
        I am ready because the Devine Devotion is all
I need.

Not Knowing

Not knowing you are there makes me weary.
Not knowing if your coming home can be a little

                                        Leary.

Not knowing how much you love me is so

                        Wrong.

Not knowing if your all mine, I can't be

                        Strong.

And not knowing how sweet you taste is far

                        Too much.

Thinking about you with someone else that

                        You will touch.

I hate not knowing that you're out there.
Makes chills go up and down all over my

                        Body everywhere.

Just keep me in mind at all times,
Because not knowing we'll be together leaves
My tears from falling from chimes.

You Know Who You Are!

This poem was written for you!
      You know who you are.
We met over many years ago.
      You know who you are.
While looking at your strong serious side,
      You know who you are.
I fell deep inside your eyes.
      You know who you are.
You asked me about me.
      You know who you are.
And I was interested in you.
      You know who you are.
Being happy at seeing you smile.
      You know who you are.
I said to myself, it's been a while.
      You know who you are.
Since I met someone so sweet.
      You know who you are.
Making me feel like falling to my feet.
      You know who you are.
Well since you do, I will remain so true
      Because this woman here really, really
Loves you.
      So you better know who you are.
My private world with a music star very
      Exclusive and extremely sharp
      In many ways you're even smart
      Loving you really pays, but not knowing
      Who you are is worth many coming days.

Your Inspiring Ways

The phone calls that I receive in the
      middle of the night, the early
part of the day or some where in the
      afternoon- is something to think
about. What you say to me is not the words, it's
      sound.
I'm feeling you baby! I'm with you in every
      motion I can describe. As soon as you
open your mouth the earth in my veins shatter.
      I shake because you have so many
inspiring ways that moves the earth.
      Your gift is most talented and chartering
like a jet with double the fuel, taking off
      the runway of my heart.
Your inspiring ways that the Spirit shot
      through you have been handed over
to me in the form of a man.
      Whenever you feel the need to need me,
love me, love someone, kiss someone, and hold
      someone, I have a bunch of all of the
above to share.
      Your inspiring ways reaches a new
dimension of light that only will shine with
      the right person.

Candle Light And Romance

Touching you baby, I know what to feel
        You move me so deeply.
I can't wait for you to come. The clock begins
        To soothe me. Are you for real?
Waiting on the right time- Oh but when is the
        Right time?
Candle light and romance in the dark is all
        We need.

Your body is so inviting to see, and the nakedness
        Of your soul is where I want to be.
When holding you so firmly, I rest my head
        So close- those lips I remember the day
You kissed me in September.
        Candle light and romance in the dark
is all we need.

Now take your hand and place it in mine.
        No need to crumble. You are so fine.
Let me light your stick in no way anyone else
        Can. I will love you forever.
        Just be my man.
        Candle light and romance in the dark is all
        We need!

<u>Dedications</u>

To all of you out there who lost
a loved one,
To the many people not here today,
    married couples all over
the world, I dedicate.

I dedicate.
    I dedicate within my heart.
I dedicate,
I dedicate throughout my soul.
I dedicate
    I dedicate to heal a broken spirit,
I dedicate,
    I dedicate to the mourners as a
               whole.
I dedicate,
I dedicate to the love in my life.
I dedicate,
    I dedicate to the man up above,
I dedicate,
    I dedicate to love not at it's best
but to keep it everlasting within.
    I dedicate,
    I dedicate to the singers and songwriters who
recognize our lost.
I dedicate,
    I dedicate to the many strong mothers and
fathers striving to make a way.
I dedicate,
I dedicate to the many emotions
that plays a part in a decision.
I dedicate,

26

I dedicate to hope, peace, and happiness
placed on the lives of those missing.

I dedicate all and every thing I have
mentioned in the above, because I know
in every living being out there, this life
of ours may not be perfect, but with the power of
thought, with the power of
proper peace, and with the power of the
almighty universe himself, that all
will prosper and heal, and love that
there may always be a dedication of
appreciation to more than one!

We are still here standing strong. Let no man take us over and
under throughout any circumstance there may be!

For the many lives lost September 11, 2001 may we remember.

A Perfect Picture

In all that you do I have placed a picture of you.
That picture fills a void that I never be annoyed.
There is so much love underneath your hidden smile.
Does not cost me anything to see you for a long while.
Many people like me do not know this perfection.
I have the upper hand in more than many will see.
Our clock has ticked to all with the right time.
But it does not matter if you can't see me and just be mine.
Let's let our spirits lead the many ways,
To love, happiness, and the forgiving of many days.
This is not a perfect picture by no means,
It is our hearts that is greater than the light that beams.
So don't, mistake anything I'm saying to you.
My perfect picture is above where the sky is blue.

<ins>*Thank You God!*</ins>

If I had to say anything it would be this.
God, you are my fortress and my soul.
　　　I have learned to carry you with me as a
whole.
　　　My life would not be complete if you were
not here.
　　　I can't even imagine waking up not being
able to cheer.
　　　You have made me who I am today!
I would not know what to do or what to say.
　　　When I walk into a cloudy room,
some how a light just seems to turn on full bloom.
　　　This little light of mines, I'm going to
Let it shine, let it shine, let it shine, let it shine.
　　　It is you who have made this real.
No one else can hand me all that you have and
　　　　　close any deal.
The love, your son, my life, all makes me complete.
　　　I am this person so very unique.
So as I walk with you daily in my heart.
　　　I will always look up to you never to be
apart.
　　　You taught me such a long time ago,
How to love another and appreciate all I know.
　　　This I learned and take with me everyday.
Because God you are so amazing no words can
　　　　　Say. Thank you!

I Bet You Didn't Know

I bet you didn't know those years ago
We would look back on the day we first met.
I bet you didn't know I had this inkling
To be more than just a friend.
I bet you didn't know I have loved you for a
Long time.
I bet you didn't know people like you motivate me.
I bet you didn't know all this time we have been
apart, I never forgot how nice of a person you are.
I bet you didn't know how much strength I have
gained making me more willing to take on a lot in my life.
I bet you didn't know there are very few people
like you who can continue to make me feel as special as you do.
Because, I know truly that you are very on point,
moving, and inspiring. Throughout these past years I have met
many others, but it was your beautiful face, smile, kiss, and hug-a-
whole that have kept me.
I want to say something to you in a whisper or two:
The price we pay to be who we are is nothing
Compared to a life long star!
I knew from day one, you had a plan.
Taking those steps, doing all you can.
Now with me, I move in a way
I know what we share is more than words
Can say!
But always remember, how close we'll be,
I bet you didn't know, both of us would exchange
that golden key.
Love is forever and will last without an end with the right person!

That Wonderful Night

When you told me that you wanted to let me see you in action, I didn't anticipate on what came about.

I tried my best to hurry and get there to be in the front, but it was hard and a lot of traffic.

Me and my girl Barbara both was so excited to see what was to be, and low and behold once I arrived to this dainty club of some sort I was so amazed by the people there to see you.

Well although it was around 8:30 or so I did not miss a thing. I heard your voice from the back but guess what I had the honor to see your beautiful picture in the front window of that dainty club. Wow!

As the music began I stood somewhere in the back and gazed with such amazement! Just to know I finally was there to watch your talented body perform was so awesome.

Then when the intro began, I must tell you chills just all of a sudden began!

Your name came out of his mouth and there you were. God bless you! So together!

Then as I watched all that I have heard you speak about such a long time ago I said to my girl, that's him!

Well let me tell you a little something: with all that you have worked on this part of my life that you share with me, has really paid off. This was such a wonderful night for me to see.

Then the after night with you at my door,
Made me want to see you perform more!
But it was a private affair at this time.
You did more than ring my chime!
I welcomed you in my world.

Bringing back those memories in a twirl.
I can truly say you are still the same.
Tossing and turning me until I came.
What a wonderful night you gave to me.
Who would have thought after 16 years
This is how it would be?

That Dashing Light

That dashing light that shines high and above the finest and most wonderful head I have ever seen.

Dashing as you are really exposing the type of man you seem to be.

Never livid or jealous without much worry in the world, ahh nice to see you in the wind as I blow my lips to you worth a thousand and one kisses or maybe just two.

That dashing light of the flame you had to put out that arose between my legs, such a raging fire.

Only you can make me so mesmerized that the loneliness that faded a long time ago moves further into another dimension, another direction, another part of this world.

That dashing light is you as you walk into the very room I first saw us make love in. Do you remember?

That dashing light has lingered throughout my journey that I may always carry it within my heart and not need a flash, or bulb because of the memories and the future of knowing your existence is forever in my life.

I Love The Way You Kiss

I love the way you kiss,
        With your tender touch
                that moves me so much.
I love the way you kiss,
        As you glide your mouth across
          my face.
                Leaving wet lips for me
          to taste.
I love the way you kiss,
        The warmth of your tongue
          inserted against mines.
             moving in and out,
        all around leaving many
          signs.
I love the way you kiss,
        When I have a chill all over,
            it makes the heat come down
              from head to shoulder.
Oh yes, I love the way you kiss,
        Our bodies match like the perfect
          heaven.
          Curling together shaped like
            the number seven.
I love the way you kiss,
        You fill my every sumptuous need,
          I start to sweat just thinking
            about your seed.
And if they're ever was a kiss like ours,
        no one can help but watch us

devour,
the pleasure of many universal souls united
in spirit.
My mouth awaits for you to come,
Just plant those beautiful babies
right here for some.
You won't be disappointed, cause I'll give
you my all,
So squeeze me tight, we're going to have a ball!
I love the way you kiss!

Irresistible Fruits

When the first day of life began, how
Would we have known the anticipation of a man and a
woman would be so real?

You see, God made this man right over
There and she over here standing diagonal, horizontal, in a circular
motion, all around each other.

The beauty that stood between them only made
things a little harder.

Man is supposed to be strong. Woman soft and
sensuous, but, from that very first day we have took another role
in life. That irresistible fruit of divine has given us more than the
juices of magic, but it has made us alert, aware, and loving.

It won't take a piece of fruit to tempt us, but to
bring joy to our hearts.

The role is on hold for right now. Strength is
about the mind and what is right for us. Man and Woman, TAKE
A BITE!

Holding On To Heaven

I walked and felt my sore feet crumple.
    Then I began to think, I have tried and
tried to keep my mind free and clear from   all that false illusion.
Temptation plays but I turn the other
        cheek!
Daily I ask God about the different walks in
        my life,
the many people who come my way, and the
        choices I make.
I don't know whether I am right or wrong in
        all I do but, he makes everything go
well.
    I am holding on to all I have been
blessed with.
    Holding on to the one, two, or maybe
three good things around me.
    Holding on to the peace I have accepted
and projected.
    I may not have much and I don't have
to be the smartest, but all I know is this:
    I am holding on to heaven as my home
To be, if there is nothing else.
Lord, I am not going to let go

It's Never To Late

I don't consider myself to be taken back by anything. I remember a long time ago when we first met there were many prayers I sent up to heaven.

In return I sat back and looked upon the hills not thinking if he would apply to all that I asked. You see when I registered my prayers to him I knew once he sent them back with a return receipt, all was well.

One of those things was to keep you as my companion for a long time. I did not anticipate that he would give me this unless it was in my best interest.

You see, God knows better than all of us. What I have learned is the magic behind belief and true faith. Both that I stand affirm in truth.

Well dear lover of mines, you were in my prayers all the time. I loved you! I love you! I always am happy to see you! And everyday I don't know what will be next but I do know this: Whether it is one day, one minute, or forever, I count the blessings that God fulfills me with. Knowing you is wonderful but having God is forever.

Don't Take It To Another Limit

Sometimes things are just not worth
The effort.
Trying times can be very rough!
Happiness is just another
Emotion.
Don't take it to another limit!
Looking your best is always
Wonderful,
But reaching over to insult the other
Is for fools.
You don't have to be discouraged by
No means at all,
Just reach up then down and say
I love you.
Don't take it to another limit!
Be the leader that you represent,
There are many fortunes to be sent.
If there was a king to be crowned
Loving you would play more than a
Frown.
So think twice before you make a false
Move.
The wait may be over so there's nothing
To prove.
Don't take it to another limit!

Soul To Soul

Reaching, climbing, touching,
    all I could feel
      of you.

Shapely and molding through
    the arch of
      our backs.
      But I connect!

Lifting to a new height,
    a new line
        straight
    or crooked, rotating
      all and about.
      But I connect!

There has to be a way for me
    to insert,
      my liberty of joy,
    on to you.

Right now my divine measure of
      love and warmth
is circulating throughout the
      pubic hairs between my legs,
my thighs, my lower body of moisture.
    Now run your imagination wild.
wilder than any cat or tiger in the
      jungle.

Faster than a spinning wheel not
    knowing how to stop.

Smell It!

It's not anyone's business
                    But ours!
                    So,
Soul to soul we will reach this
                    passion.
Soul to soul is inspired by
                    truth.
Soul to soul is recognized by living
                    a whole.
Soul to soul is our universal and us
                    connection
                    becoming

1

If I Catch You

If I catch you I am sure you will
            be free!
Free to absorb and soak up the
        love spilled on to your collar.
If I catch you, there would be no
            need to be alone.
So much happiness would occur that
        you wouldn't be able to face
                anything else.
If I catch you, I would cuddle,
        huddle, caress, and undress the
                nakedness of your dreams.
If I catch you, this little bit of leeriness
        that may be in your subconscious
                    mind
would be gone forever.
        I am awaiting, I am looking, I
have my arms out, I am ready!
        Ready to be with you, to love you,
to hold you, to tear that hype of inside
        happiness into pieces of
                gummy drops.
There is a brand new woman in the front
        line of your life.
And she is another part of your destiny!
        Another part of your future!
She is your undeniable other half!
        So if I catch you,
let us be joined where no man
        can take us apart!

<u>Waiting</u>

It's not cool to keep her waiting.
    You said you would call.
She expected to see you soon.
    But when is soon to you?
Tomorrow, today, yesterday,
      When?
Maybe timing crossed another
    Path.
Was there some type of misunder-
    Standing?
I bet you don't even feel the need to
    Explain.
Well listen carefully to me brother.
    This sister here has heard it
      All!
There ain't no way you can get out
    Of this one.
It only takes a little care.
    I've seen many faces,
And been a whole lot of places,
    So what you think you know
Is your own selfish dream.
    My God above never lets me
Wait.
He loves me! He taught me! He
    Healed me!

43

So keep in mind that all you do,
     May hurt some or maybe few.
But this chick over here,
     Keeps her mind free
And clear.
     For love of herself
Only on top shelf.
     Cause when the time comes,
It will be you waiting along with
          Those other bums!

Chocolate Cake With Strawberries On Top!

Nice to know how sweet you are!
Holding each other close and never far.
As I checked you out up and down,
my body trembles all over and around.
The blackness of your skin that is
on display has such sex appeal,
I get choked up thinking about
the way you feel.
But as I sit down and think of the
moments we share,
I see your handsome face looking at me
as I stare.
Chocolate cake with strawberries on top
is what I see!
with whip cream drizzling down my
mouth is where your lips should
be!
I know for sure, there's only one cure.
The love I have inside my heart,
came about the moment we decided to
start.
The romance keep tasting as sweet as
Cherry pie,
Because there's no other like you,
my kind of guy!
Chocolate cake with strawberries on top
is my favorite desert.
Can't wait until I eat you, promise it
won't hurt.

I'll nibble the affection right on point.
　　Then you will lay back
And want to smoke a joint!
　　But it is me who will be the one
To get you high,
　　So let's stop talking and give it a
　　　　Try.
Chocolate cake with strawberries on top
　　Is your body moving in motion,
Waiting for me to sop up all that
　　　　Devotion!

Just Be Honest With Me!

I know it is hard for many to say
    What may be.
But, first and foremost is honesty.
    There is no trust when you
Are not for real.
    Take my advice and let me
Know the deal.
    The worst thing that can
Happen is I go my way.
    That's better than me
Having the wrong thing to say.
    Life is short without a doubt.
In all situations I no my way out.
    There is enough hurt and pain
Already in my heart.
    So why would you want to
Add more, just to play the part?
    You know I am so outraged
By what you did.
    I am an adult, not some little
    Kid.
Sixteen years thinking I knew you
    Well,
Huh, you just showed me, so
    You too can go to hell!
But one thing I would like to see,
    No matter what, just be
Honest with me!

<u>Don't Touch My S---!</u>

Whatever you do, don't touch my s---!
        I put it there for me and not
For you to take hold of it.
        I respect your ---t, you better
Respect mines.
        It does not matter what kind
Of s--- it is, just keep your hands off of
        It.
He's mines, that's mines, I live here
      You go over the other way,
But just don't touch my s---!
    My s--- is golden, my s--- is
Unique, and my s--- is my s---,
    So whatever you do, don't
Touch my ---t!

<u>Sonia & Ivan</u>

Amazingly enough she was strong
In all her ways to not give in to what seemed to be everlasting. But
as the time grew on she realizes that better days were coming.
So freaky but funky was to be in store
For her.
Here he comes, tall, black, and right on time.
He showed her long ago that he was the one.
But the universe holds many signals for us to
read. Oh how beautiful they are!
Inspiring, yes a true romance needed to be read.
Her name is Sonia and his is Ivan,
Not just a cute couple of names that combined to one, but
One of my greatest love stories needed to
Be told.
Well here I say, to this day,
When things go short,
And your life can't be sort,
There's a strong type of force
That will throw you off
That certain course,
Our life seem still,
With no one to share
Not even a Bill,
Then guess what comes about
Tall, short, skinny, or stout
It is he who is brought to she
And Ivan brought to Sonia!

I Love Him!

October 10, 1998, you walked into my life
    So magical,
Throughout 1999 was a struggle, did not
    Know if I could do it anymore.
2000 seemed like the final point in our lives.
    I did not know if I could love you
Anymore, but I did.
    I loved you until it hurt.
Could I accept all to go with this picture?
    I thought I could but little did
I know.
    My heart was beating but I felt
Dead.
    How did I allow this to get that
Way?
    How did I let you turn me out
Where I wake up with that thing on my
    Mind?
You worked it, you looked at it, you
Touched my every whim of suggestion in
    My mind.
You taunted me with your lips, your desire,
    Your movements and most of all,
        YOUR LOVE!
I know it hurt, I felt the pain, I was there,
    But you, you, you, are this pleasure
Principle to my erogenous zone that
    Appeared so many years ago.
Now I know things are not perfect,
    I don't expect you to feel the same,
But you do!
    What I realize is the power of our love

Is so strong, so dynamic and most
 Sensational that no man or woman will
Take us under.
 Different things have come and went,
But our love stood in the middle standing
 Just as straight as the arrow that a
Cupid points to the heart.
 I love you, and I will shout it out to the
World.
 Now, we have approached the year
2002, and like fire as hot as we are, our
 love is still in full flame!
Know this, you this man I call my man,
 I will open up the doors to my legs
My heart, and my mind to all that is to be
 Because I know you are amazing to
 ME!

Something Sensuous Is,

Something sensuous is you,
Peeling an orange then biting
     Into it,
And I, wanting to lap up
     All the juice,
    Around you're beautiful
      lips!

Something sensuous is reading
    A romance novel
     And you
Pouncing on me like one
    of the characters.

Something sensuous is a
      train
coming into the station
    and your face
      is all
       I
     see, when
the doors finally open!

Something sensuous is
    how I imagine
walking to another
    part of this universe,
and there awaits the love letter
    you wrote me a long time
     ago.

Something sensuous is all the

anger we share,
turning into
chocolate covered cherries
on top of us while we make
love.

But what can be more sensuous
than pure sweet satisfying
Love, oh love the way it should
Be represented.

In every hand that dishes out some
dirt is a clean one,
We will learn to understand that
Being sensuous is a given.

Something sensuous is all of the
Above, because it is real.
Real to me, to you and to all who
Believe in pure sensuality!

A'

I had a vision long ago
Of someone special entering my life.
As it turned out, many
People tried to enter the womb of my
Heart,
But that certain force pushes them back in time.
Then one day,
When I leased expected it came this guy.
He had the most stunning eyes.
They were kind of glassy. He had a little
Jive to him, but cute as can be.
He warmed my heart the very
Moment I saw him because of his
Approach. I like that!
He knew what he saw he wanted,
Me!
I wasn't sure if I wanted him but
What I know now is
After all this time, if I couldn't
Figure out the place this man
Belonged, I found it.
That is with me!
A', such a sweet name
For such a wonderful
Lady.
No A', you don't deserve me! That's
why you don't have me!
Anymore!

Just A Big Ole Piece Of Sweet Potato Pie!

Yeah, that's you! When I think of
The holidays, I look back
On what we usually have for
Desert.
However it would be nice one day
To have you.
All your sweetness is the sugar
And syrup that is mixed in
As the beginning ingredients.
Then I add some of your finesse
Like nutmeg, and cinnamon
Which is your personality!
That huskiness you carry is the
Potatoes nice and large.
Then it would not be as creamy without
The dreaminess of your eyes,
Which is represented by the milk.
A pinch of spice here and there is your
Sense of humor, which really is
What makes this taste good!
As I fill my shell up with you
In the middle to the top, I bake you
In my oven of warmth just
Enough to heat to perfection.
When you have cooked, I know I have won the contest
For this prize, because you are
Just a Big Ole Piece of Sweet Potato Pie!

I Do, But Won't

I do love you,
    But won't make a fool
Of myself.

I do want to spend my life with
    You,
    But won't wait around until
Your ready.

I do have great expectations,
    But won't insert them on
You.

I do love to make beautiful
    Romance,
But won't over do it by smothering
    You.

I do seek another side to this
    Relationship,
But won't give up!

I do expect the same respect
    As I give,
But won't put you on lock
    Down to get it.

I do want our love to last,
    But won't chase you around
For it.

And if all my do's work for us,
    And won't never have to
Become,
Then the preacher can one day
    Pronounce us man and wife.

I will kiss you now!

Nickels From The Sky

    Every penny that drops lands
Somewhere free.

As I pick them up one by one
remember that saying:
> See a penny
> Pick it up
> All the days
> You'll have
> Good luck!

Well I know, not only the pennies
On the ground, my luck is having you
All around.

So please remember this:
> Every nickel that
> Comes your way.
> Is just me here
> To say,
> Your touch is so
> Very rare,
> Having you is
> More than I
> Could bare.
> But a nickel from
> The sky,
> Is Gods embrace
> Full and high.
> The richness in
> This money,
> Means more to me
> Than the taste of

Honey.
Every nickel that
Falls,
Starts the love and
The calls,
But it does not take a coin to come
From heaven.
The starting match is more than
Seven.
Two people in love make it
Whole.
So spread the word and live the
Role.
Just catch those nickels from the
Sky,
And you'll never ever have to say
Good-bye!

I Ordered That!

As I Rome through this catalog of
    Mines,
I see the many different items that
    Remind me of you.
The red dress with the slit high enough
    For your hands to slide up my
        Thighs,
So I ordered that!

The sexy telephone that helps me reach
    Out and touch someone, that is
      You!
    I ordered that!

The wonderful frame that will sit on
    My desk as I look at your
    Beautiful picture,
I ordered that!

A nice pair of pumps, with a heel very
    Tall and stimulating to the eye.
      I ordered that!

Page by page I turned to something
    That comes across the way I see
You and how wonderful you are.
    But you see, there is so much in
      This book that reminds me

Of the many different and sensual
    Ways of you and how I want to
Soothe you, caress you, and stroke you.
    I want to just show you how much
I adore you!
So if I have to order anything else, I
    Hope it's your heart!

If I Allow You,

If I allow you to take over
What is mines, I will lose control of
My property.
If I allow you to choose who
Should be in my life, I would not
Have any friends.
If I allow you to make all of
the decisions for me, my choices would
be limited.
If I allow you to love me where I
Can't determine it from hate, the abuse
Will continue.
If I allow you to form your own
Type of discipline to my kids which
Always make them cry,
What kind of mother would I be?
So, remember this: As a woman,
I have a choice. For something to be or
Not!
If I allow you to take over my
Overall being, WHO AM I?
Always know that the kingdom
Of God resides within!
So, that will never happen!

A Change Of You

A change in the season would be most
     Inviting to our bodies
Because we dress according to the
        Weather.

A change in clothing is nice for
    those of us who want to
Stay in tact with our
     self image.

A change in our habits makes
Us move on to something
      Different.

A change in our environment
    Helps to open up a
Different surrounding.

But, a change of you can't be
    Replaced. You are who
God made you to be. I love
    You just the way you are!

Part Two Of This Journey!

If you are enjoying a relationship with someone special in your life, that is more than a lot of people. There is so much love out there for the right person to come upon. I would like to reach out to the many ladies and gentlemen who have a hard time finding the "quote on quote" right person.

Love is an extraordinary thing when recognized and appreciated by the right people involved. I write about love because we are all love. It does not take a miracle to dig deep within our own selfishness to find what someone may be searching for. My poetry reaches out to many lovers out there. The chocolate side of magic is in between that sweet apple pie of your soul, but the look of birth. You just want to relax and take in the warmth of the wind. You want to allow the sun to peak at you in a way that no one else can. So, you tilt back on this magic carpet of love as he takes a bite of that mint intellect that makes you want to grab whole real tight.

I want all of you lovers or even someone who wants to be loved in the right way in the right places to lay back and imagine this for a bit:

You are on this desert island with nothing but the sand. With a broad and awakening smile in your heart with such loving suggestions from your Spirit, you look back on what once was. You can't help but grin because it was one of those everlasting moments that cannot be replaced or changed. Maybe it was the new dress that had a deep neckline that made him plunged his lips into your neck and suck up your sweetness. Or maybe it was those jeans that fit your butt so tight but not tacky that made her surround you and just grabs your ass. Think about it! Memories so set back in your mind that you can take it to another level in your life. Sometimes things are not what we want them to be for the moment, however a little temporary look back into what was at some point and time is most magnificent.

If I could give anything of myself to all of you wonderful people who have taken the time out to look into something God helped me create, then I would like to share some of me with you. My poetry is for the lover in you, in her, in he, and in all of us. Allow it to take you to another place for whatever time period you would like it to be. Then after it takes you there, bring that special someone with you.

Let him or her share and taste this butter together with you.

Soft, sultry, tasty, and most sensual ways to get in between the sheets. Work it out and work it in. Whatever suits you just do it. Make love into pure happiness at the rate of words. Magic is in the air for everyone so, don't let anything steal your joy. You will find it! It is right around the corner.

I love you all,

"inspiration"

Nasty Thing In You

One day after you opened up the doors
To my womanhood,
I looked the other way while staring at
you. I saw right through every
inch of your vein.
I smiled, because I realized that I just
finished with this full course meal,
YOU!
The desire that was left inside my
mouth was more than
I hungered in the beginning.
So I reached down into
my imaginary purse covered with
pubic hairs, and touched
myself.
As you looked back at me, I notice
such inviting suggestions saying to me
Come get it!
So I did! Umm so sweet, so delectable
And so wild.
I just love that nasty thing in you!

Everything About You!

There is so much that I want to
    Say,
But can't get it out!
    Your face, so sweet with lips
Soooo soft, and eyes that make me melt.
    It's everything about you!
Not only the way you kiss me and
    Hold my body
Close to yours,
    It's everything about you!
Not just the way you treat me,
    Just like a queen on a throne.
    It's everything about you!
And how you run your fingers down
    My spine
    Into my mind,
As my skin tingles from excitement!
    It's everything about you!
You are a man who shows every bit
    Of his nature.
Well spoken, well hung, and so
    Masculine abroad!
    It's everything about you!
So, don't forget what I'm about to say,
    I have loved you from the
    Very first day.
When we spoke on the telephone
    You had this deep undertone.

I did not imagine it would be this good
    When I'm in your arms,
I feel like a woman should.
    Moving our bodies with all
Kinds of motion.
    Can't help but give you all
Of my devotion.
    That's why it's not only one,
Or even two.
    It's everything about you!

I Can't Stop Wanting It,

Steamy nights go by every time I cry.
I pull the pillow close to me
And all I see.
It's you,
All I smell,
It's every moment to tell,
What I feel
And
That is a sensitive touch when you kneel.
I saw your face right below
My waist.
Then I grabbed you by the way, without
Anything to say.
You said, breathe baby just breathe, and
A sigh of relief came unto me.

You see, I can't stop wanting it,
I can't stop loving this good shit,
I can't stop soaking you up in my love.
The diamonds and pearls mean
Nothing in a snow branch that you shove.

But you put it on me, like no other
Has.
I can't even sleep without another
Challenging task.
Those inviting thoughts that enters
My mind,
Has been taken over by all that was
Left behind.
I just can't stop wanting it.

<u>*I'm Gonna Try To*</u>

I'm gonna try to do all the things for you that a woman should.

I'm gonna try to give every bit of care for the love I have installed.

I'm gonna try to hold on to the promises we made together.

I'm gonna try to be the entire woman you will always need.

I know you will trust our love and be all we can together.

I'm gonna try to build a life with structure added without doubt.

I'm gonna try to maintain all that could be of who I am from head to toe.

Listen to me carefully: Being this woman here, standing in the front line to happiness, if you want me, I will be there every way possible. My love never tells a lie only the truth. So, no matter what:

I'm gonna try to do what is real in all of my soul to lift that hidden light in yours

<u>When I Pull On You,</u>

When I pull on you, it will be noticed!
The way I grab and hold tight to the
      Strength of your muscles.
When I pull on you, your eyes will
Close slowly while thinking how good
      This feel!
When I pull on you, your mouth will
Open a little bit, because of how deep
      You are breathing.
When I pull on you, the sweat builds
On your forehead and triggles down
      Onto your stomach.
And as I continue to pull,
You tighten your legs, and then hold them
Straight out, with glory of anticipation.
When I pull on you, I know you
Will invite my mouth to join, and as
I bring my lips closer to the tip,
Your body trembles as you look
      Down at me. Then!!!!!
When I pull on you harder
I'll say WAKE UP!!
IT WAS ONLY A DREAM

<u>A Picture Speaks A Thousand Words</u>

I was sitting here gazing at a picture I took of you just a few days ago.

OH what a Beautiful Face!
Now, I could look at you all day long.
That mouth, those lips and glittering eyes,
My God you look good!
Such a handsome person you are, with a face that tells so much.
I know why I fell for you.
Just before I took that picture, we made love over and over again.
The sign of exhaustion showed in your eyes but the look of desire still played the part.
I could hold you all day and kiss you on those beautiful babies. I would tell you how much I adore you.
But I don't have to at this moment, because I
Know this: In my heart and my soul all I see in that picture is who you are. So good and so wonderful, I know for sure A Picture speaks a thousand words.

An Umbrella Of Romance

Finding you is the best thing to happen to me.
When I wake up next to you, your smile
       Is all I see.
The heart inside is filled with joy.
You'r all man, not some toy.
We have come very far by the touch of grace.
The time flies by without a trace.
But the best I know loves you,
Deep in my heart you will always be
       My boo.!
As I take a stand for all I got,
I'll always remember, you are so hot.
Now when we step out in the rain.
You hold me so tight, there's more to gain
But my fire of desire will always enhance.
The love we share is an umbrella of
       Romance!

Part Three Of This Journey!

The following pages are dedicated to the one person that has been behind me 110%. Without the trust and faith he had in me, I would not be able to proceed with any of this. So I open up this section to my only true love and never forsaken part of this journey I'm on called life. It is He who has guided me to the unlimited source of abilities. It is He who put the pen and paper in my hand, in front of me and saw to it that I begin. He appointed the Holy Spirit to me and asks that I understand what he is trying to do for me. Without question of all his goodness I could only say, thank you.

It is very important to me that I say all of this to you who is reading. The possibilities are endless out there. God is all over us and we need to abide his will. The significant part of living is making everyday worth the while. If it weren't for he, I would not be as far as I am. So I want to say thank you! Thank you!

I dedicate these special poems to you God, The one I love.

You Believed in Me

The days I thought to myself about
    What I was not and who
    hould I be, was long ago.
I looked upon the heavens in the hills
    And grasp whole to a soul that
Appeared before my eyes.
    I awakened to some type of
Vision that I thought was just an
Illusion. It was my faith!
    I remembered a prayer some
Time back that I made towards the
    Stars.
I was young at the time, but I believed
That all was possible.
    And it was,
Thirty some odd years later here I am.
Facing challenges that were worth the wait
Despite the fact that I was a child in need
Of a friend.
    What a friend we have in Jesus
I used to sing in church.
    But it was not the fact that he was
My friend,
    God appointed him for us.
And he has proven his love to me.
    You see He believed in me!
And the trust I gained for myself has
    Met in the eyes and the power of
It all that I can say THANK YOU
    Aloud and clear.
Thank you because you believed in me.

Through Each Test

Through each test I stood still.
Through each test I had to wait.
Through each test there was
                    a cause
Through each test my value got
                        Higher.
Through each test I began to
                        Understand.
Through each test I became
                    New.
Through each test I learned.
Through each test there was
                    A fact.
Through each test there was
                    An outcome.
Now as I finish this portion of
This test I will await the
                        Result.
Because through every test there
Are soft reproductions.

I Depend on You

When I wake up, I depend on you.
When I go to sleep, I depend on you.
When I leave for work, I depend
On you.
When I arrive home, I depend on you.
When I feed my children, I depend
on you.
When my children are hungry, I
Depend on you.
When I need to be loved, I depend on
You.
When I am already loved, I depend
On you.
When I come into an inheritance, I
Depend on you.
When it comes time to spend it, I
Depend on you.
I depend on you Lord for everything!
I know without you I cannot wake up!
I know without you I cannot go to sleep!
I know without you I cannot go to work!
I know without you I cannot arrive home!
I know without you I cannot feed my kids!
I know without you my kids will starve!
I know without you I can't experience real
Love!
I know without you, I am not loved!
I know without you, I would not have
Come into any type of money!
And I know without you I would not know
How to spend any money I depend on you, My God for
Everything!

If Every Child Knew You

Sometime I sit and listen to what other people say about their life. I look into what they are saying and I wonder to myself, are they for real? This part of this journey we call life is so important to all of us. I know some of us do not understand but let me explain it just a bit. This great big world we were born over and over again unto, has been a twirl or two for some of us but I don't think we all know how important it is for us to be a part of. We are children of God! Oh how sweet it sounds to be a child of the magnificent one. If every child of his knew the power that resides is so wonderful. If every child knew what each one of us represented and believed. If every child knew what he or she meant to him. If every child knew what value they are to each one of us. We are a oneness; we are united in peace if we allow our spirits to be met at the right time. If every child knew who you are to this world it would be a wonderful adventure for all of us.

My Hero

I listen to people talking about those people
Who helped the others by sacrificing their
Lives to rescue others.

I look at people who worship individuals
Because they preach the "Holy Word"

I observe others who take a bow to someone
Who wears a crown.

I watch many as they salute someone in
A pacific uniform represented the United
States.

I listen to how people sing the praises
Of another who maybe, is successful
Because the art they were born to do.

But within all of these people goes one
Thing they may or may not have done or
Do. Or maybe they were born to wear
A crown or decided a long time ago they
Will read the words of the bible throughout
To many listening. Or they have this talent
They went to school for.
Maybe their jobs are permitted to run in and
Out of burning buildings that may be falling.
Just remember this: None of the above would
Be possible for any of them if it wasn't for
That certain somebody.
No one would be able to do all those
Magnificent things that we seemed to forget

Where it came from because we get caught
Up in the motion by the emotions.
All that was, is and will ever be is because
Of him.

       Him, and you say whom? The
maker of you.
The same person who made the buildings that
Someone decided to blow up or burn down.
The same person who grace the mother of
The one you cherish because he saved your
Son/daughter.
Him, the one who made it possible for you to
Kneel to the one who wears the crown
Him, the one who made it possible for that
Person you salute to walk with honors.
Him, who sent out the words for the
Preacher,
To be able to speak to you on a Sunday,
Monday ect.
Him, him, him,
Now tell me, who is the real hero?
I know who it is and his name is Jesus!
Because we know without our heavenly
Father above, even he would not be possible.
So. Without he we are not possible.
    Think about it!

Part Four Of This Journey!

In every passage of our lives the experience of newness is always inviting to the soul. As I keep the paste going I will eventually reach a height of new ground with others. I am allowing all of you into my secret world of peace and love at every given moment. The test to show all of you the true side of my Poetry! Now I will lead you back into that sultry world that has to end for our own good. I know a lot of you can relate to this,

Romance. Here I go again to this quite side of madness of sensuality. As he enters your world, he rotates his body to the level of understanding that only you can adapt to. Their secrets that meet each other's eye are what's so magnificent to both their mental wariness.

Hot, steamy, love, that is what it is all about. Reach higher and higher until you get there and go for it. Now dig a little deeper into the next part of this adventure. This is for the love that we hurt. The pain that came from loving someone, as well as the reprocution behind it. Most of us know what I am talking about, so let us take this part to a different level of our love that we can't understand WHY WE HURT?

<u>We Have Been Through This Before,</u>
<u>Now It's Time to Move On</u>

All I search for in life with someone is what
    We can share of each other.
When times get tough, we try to work it out.
    Some days I just don't know what
        To do!
Every moment over and over is wonderful
    With you at the time.
Many others have dreamed of what it would
    Be like to have the romance, the
Intensity, the love, the passion that keeps
    Us both so alive.
If only I kept my guards up, it would not
    Hurt so badly.
Falling into your arms night after night I
    Loss myself.
I thought we would go the long haul.
    But, whom was I kidding?
I believed in you fully in my heart.
    And even as I write this poem it
        Hurts.
But I believe in telling what it's all about
    So the next one will be secure.
I'm sorry this is how it has to end but,
The things you say. The way you show
Your true self, blurting out words that hurt.
    Really is what took the cake.
Just remember this:
        A Good Woman comes across
        So very rare.
        You will have a hard time trying
        To find out if she really care.

In every given moment true love
Can last.
Doesn't happen over night
Cause that's to fast.
learning to trust someone has to
Be.
I think I have shown you that,
Can't you see?
When you play with any feelings
You will always lose.
Go ahead and do it,
But time will choose.
It is YOU that will hurt and feel
insane.
I don't have to do anything.
You are already in pain.
What you put out, you will
Receive.
That's just pure karma
You will achieve.
So don't think it's over just for me,
Hell is freezing right now in
        Your own dynasty.
We have been through this before,
Now it is time to move on.
Because I know I am sick of
Playing this same old song!

That Last Kiss

I don't plan to look you in the eye
Just to say something neither one of
us expect.
I am learning to do what is right
For me.
When there is another in your life,
There is no happy ending.
You see, some people are in straight
Denial about all situations.
    At the time it is
happening we can't see
What is wrong.
The emotions play a role we believe in
     Cause that's all we
have at the moment.
Seek into yourself for the truth.
It always helps.
I kissed you over and over again.
     Feeling the softness
because I thought
It was all about love.
     Then one day things
changed, your kiss
Was not soft anymore.
There was a difference!
You had withdrawn from me.
Suddenly I realized that the power
Was dying down.
I did not want to face that this is what
Was going on, but I had to.
I walked away,
That was the last kiss!

True Freedom

As the days are gone I have written to
    Myself all about me.
I started thinking what is the best way
    This life of mines should be?
Then came the wind of justice in-between
    The love in my heart and silence
Appeared in the form of truth.
    I couldn't think straight because
Of the cloudiness in front of the waves
    Towards my thoughts so, I sat
Down for the moment to analyze me.
    I looked up to God as always
For the answers and said "take me
    To the promise land of truth"
I waited just a moment and then allowed
    The flush of wind to circulate
Throughout my body.
    As I freshened up a bit and stood
With a smile on my face, I knew the
    Evening sun had appeared through
My dark eyes that cried most of the time.
    We all hurt one way or another
But when the truth seeps in our pours,
    The freedom follows,
Our freedom. Freedom to make choices,
Freedom to move forward, and freedom to
    Live the life of blissful love.
choose true freedom because that is where
    My soul lies.

After the Pain

Now that I have reserved myself all over
   Again, I realize what I should be.
I made the choice to go ahead and touch
   Another's womb and help them
Along the way.
   I talked to many others about what I
Experienced just for an opinion or so.
   But that I guess was just to ease
The soreness in my throat that tickled in
   A strange way.
After the pain of losing myself to what I
   Thought was love, had to start
A new beginning for me.
   After the pain I took the next step
Out of that so-called fantasy I lived.
   After the pain I said who am I
Kidding? I was the fool.
   After the pain I listened to that
Song by Mary and new how to relate.
   I agree with all the words,
She had to sing.
   I understand because I too want
No More Drama!

Love Never Hurts!

I remember the time when I laid there
listening to you as you talk about all
you had, and at that time I didn't.
   It always seemed that right
After we so called made love, you decided
   to drop some type of news on me.
One day you told me, well I can't see you
   for a few days because I have to take
a sperm test. You know we want to have a
    baby!
That was you and she!
   Then, you told me again
that you and she were going to get back
   together. After leading me to believe
you wanted her to leave you.
   Oh, but what about when you thought
to let me know you two were buying a home.
I don't know what your concept on love
    Is, but I know for sure
That Love does not hurt!
   So when you say you love somebody,
Please know the definition.
Remember that love don't love nobody
Especially the kind that you display.
But the roots have turned back on you!
Love does not hurt, but the pain of what you shed to me I have
flicked back on you!

Your New Living of Kitchen Hell

I still regret the day when it all came about that we were together. Think about it! When you decided to stay, What do you think was her plan?

She told you she would never let you go!

Well, if you can't see it, let me guide you through the channels:

Are you ready?

She found out about your affair, and you told her to leave because you loved another.

She refused, and said she will never let you go, NO MATTER WHAT!

She convinced you to stay by putting a guilt trip on you. Did you not know she had a plan?

Then, as she let you think she had your trust again, she bought you a new band as a symbol that you were back together and everyone can see!

It did not work! You wanted someone else! Next, she demanded to see your cell phone bill every month.

Another number was on it, so she stopped You from calling on YOUR OWN CELL!

Then, as you once again got comfortable with the other woman, she found out you called her again! So, you got scared and decided to stop all together calling on the cell.

Nothing stopped you from seeing the other, So, what does that tell you?

You have been sick for over 4 months! Back in the doctors office over and over again! They say, nothing is wrong as far as they could see.

Now bumps have broken up all around your back!

She tells you that she wants to buy a home, so, she puts money down on it for both of you.

You have gotten so scared of her that even you don't know what is going on.

Well, let me break it down to you like this.
Did you think she wanted you back just to twittle with you?

Every woman does not like to be hurt! She may have taken you back, but trust me; you are no good at this time for Any woman! She saw to that!

So suffer, my little boy. You have lost being a MAN!

I'm Not Going to Loose My Mind

Just yesterday you let me know where
  I stood.
Not above, but under where I did not expect
  To be found.
All I needed was the truth! Not in the
  Fashion you gave it to me!
You see, I'm not going to loose my mind over
  What you do!
I'm not going to loose my mind because you
  Pretended to love me!
I'm not going to loose my mind for any
  Ignorance that may be blissed
  Upon you!
I am a woman who represents
  STRENGTH, LOVE,
  AND APPRECIATION!
My soul is what kept me alive, with the
  Spirits guidance.
I know that no matter what the cost may be, I AM I!
Therefore, I am not going to loose my mind
  For the injustice that have occurred
  Throughout my heart!
You will never find another one like me!
  I am so real, and so loved by the God
  Above,
That all I am, was, and will ever be, is the
  Makings of this person called
  SELF!

Never Gonna Be the Same!

After I leave your ass you will see
The pain you have cause me!

Calling, Texting, showing I cared
You, No courtousy, so unfare

When I decide to go and stay
Finally you will see the price you pay

The thoughts you had of me 4 years ago
Have finally come to me as a NO Show

I am tired of being number two
It's not worth what you put me through

Excuse after excuse is all you do
At this point, I can't even love you

I will never understand why you came for me
4 years ago, was a waste of time today I see

If this person makes you happy, then stay
I am tired of your bullshit, because it is not
Ok!
Just know as I leave there will be some pain
Because things with you and me
Will never be the same! Now that's GAME!

How Dare You!!!

After I told you that I could not bare another heartache, you begged me to see what a real man is.

The first year was hectic but our Communication was there. You allowed me to see the fake side of you!

I saw a friendship that was so good for me. We talked, laughed and what I felt had much in common.

The one thing I did not see, is that true ugly side of you. How dare you? Take all of who I and God built up to be; turn it upside down to make YOU feel better.

Everything I said to you was true! You know that! Not telephoning me for three to four days, and I'm not supposed to question that? What's wrong with you?

The fact that you seemed so compassionate about all the things I went through with my ex, but here you are worst!

Yes, and all the short cummings that you said I had the night supposedly Valentines Day! Tell me something, how many short Cummings do I have? Do you need me to count how many you have?

Let me explain a few, if you don't know! I truly understand why the woman that was in your life decided to cheat with someone else. You have some physical short cummings that would make any woman do that. You can't satisfy her or me. I tolerated this because I thought you were a REAL MAN. My fault, I should have looked down below your waist, the answer was right there. So, how dare you?

The fact that you were not passionate did not help either. Here I am, a loving and beautiful creature recognized by many out there, and you, the one I fell for could not even make love to me the way I needed! Yet have all the mouth when it comes to trying to tell a woman off. You should have used that mouth for something else; to compensate for what was missing on you!

I don't need to be told off, I have done nothing wrong but put up with you. Someone that did not even deserve me. I let you sway me into thinking you were a better person than anyone else, but was I wrong? But I see the light now, and it definitely is not shining on you.

So how dare you! How dare you try to make me feel less than the woman I am? In all actuality you can't, because I am still and will be empowered by a better force than you, that resides up above who does not try to control me and truly see me as the child of God that I am.

Part Five Of This Journey!

Now is the time to wake up to a new beginning! I have freshened up just a bit and relaxed my mind a little, leaving all that bad ---bull---- behind! Let's start anew and remember what I was talking about before. We have washed our minds, body, and souls, into a clean water of newness. All that happened before is done! We can't changed the past, but look into a new a brighter future. An improve future of hope, fasting, and moving forward in a way only we can adjust. Now remember this is not about dial up TV, it's about you now. So this section was created to loving YOU!

I want to tell you a little something about you! Just in case you have not heard it before, I want to enlighten all of you to this. As I walk through the body of integrity, there are so many forms of fashion that represents another that we can't keep our minds on us. Now this is really what it's all about. Keeping our minds on US.
Read on a little and captivate what you did not know you even had.

This is dedicated to the one's I love for me and me alone!

This Incredible Woman!

She's more than the average but,
Never less than magnificent!

This incredible woman!

Tall, short, vivacious, luscious, and
All the trimmings a man could peak at!

This incredible woman!

Vary talented is she and smart as a whip.
She doesn't take much nonsense.
You must come clean to her!

This incredible woman!

A tad bit shy, only when necessary.
Overall she's aggressive!

This incredible woman!

Not ashamed of where she's been,
But surely knows where she's going,
And stands firmly where she's!

This incredible woman!

Her children are her world, as she
Teaches them daily about love and still
Maintains the heart of the home, with a
Full time, part time extraordinary schedule
Which gives her power and triumph,

Although she's tired!
This incredible woman!

Her man, he's never dissatisfied when he
Licks his lips of pleasure principles she
Accompanied him with before, during, and
After their romance.
Oh yeah she's sweet, all the more reason
He loves her!

This incredible woman!

Performing her best is what she does.
She believes in it all and those who doubt
Her, just don't know how amazing she can
Be!

This incredible woman is all the hard
Working sisters, mothers, grandmothers,
And daughters of our culture. We are
Exceptional, we are beautiful, and we are
A oneness ready to take on the world~

You see, God blessed us in many ways
With the features of our late ancestors on
Point to enhance others soul.

So here we are, Just Incredible!

I was designed to Fit You!

Being 5'8 with such a overly formed fit
                    Body,
Nice waist, big boobies, and extremely large
                    Butt,
And thighs I have a lot of class and style.
Writing is a MUST for me, as I extend it
                    Out to you.
All there is in my heart is LOVE.
Love in the right way, is what I want.
My children's desire is my desire.
How about you?
What is it that you want?
I mean, are you sure of yourself?
Are you responsible?
Have real love in your heart?
                    And soul?
Is making yourself happy more important
                    than anyone else?
Are you independent with a strong mind?
If all is well with you on all of these things,
Then I was designed to fit you.
We have not met before and probably
Won't at this time, but know this:
My mind is free and my heart is strong!
However has weakened a bit from hurt and
                    A lot of nonsense!
But true love is still available for you!
So don't hesitate to search a little.
Far and beyond the point of no return.
I am here! Your destiny that will be.
When the time is right in Gods eyes and his
                    Eyes only! Amen

I Am the Only Woman

You knew the first day we met, you
could love me!
It did not matter who you went home
to, every night.
It did not matter that you made the
mistake and got more involved with,
her a few months
before we came about.
You know, as soon as you saw me,
It was all over for her and just beginning
for us!
      I know it is hard to face, but the truth hurts!
I know you feel that you owe her for all
she has done for you. However,
I am the ONLY Woman for you!
Can't you see?
Every time I try to leave, you can't take it!
I am the earth of your Godliness holding
you still. I know this because you can't
function if I am gone.
Our veins have united almost 4 years ago
making the blood run deeper than anyone
else.
      Do you think it means something because you
chose to stay with her?
I am the ONLY Woman for you!
When you are with her, whether at home
or, anywhere else, it is me that you taste!
      If and when you kiss her, the moisture from
your lips is from my heavenly womanhood
      of enlightment that you share with me when
sliding deep down into my magical inner

world of excitement.
If and when you have Sex with her, it is my
name you call out in your dreams because
 we are making love!
Your manhood, has my lipstick tattooed all
over the tip.
I am the ONLY Woman for you!
You may want to deny it, to cover for her,
that is not LOVE. I know this! What she
did for you over 11 years ago was special.
      Pulling you out of the situations you were in
Sticking by you when you needed most. I
Applaud it all, but, things change, and so
do people.
Now is today and yesterday was then.
And you were a child, but what is to be
will be. Can't you see?
I have come into your life for reasons
now, so remember all I say:
I know a lot about you!
Our love goes to deep and to
intense for me not to know.
You keep coming back because it's real!
You stay with her because it's loyalty!
But one day soon, you will realize the
power that is met between us!
I don't have to say, or do anything,
It won't take a new band that she
bought!
Because you lost the other, and this
will prove you are committed to her.
It won't take checking your cell
phone bill every month for familiar
calls that you make at least 5 times
a day that she notice.

It won't take buying a house to
keep you so you can be happy and
more comfortable to want to be home.
it won't take calling you often
to keep track of where you are.
Ah ah, I don't have to do anything
But be I!
Because I am the ONLY Woman
For you!
I am always on your mind, in your dreams
And in your heart.
I am in your soul, we are programmed to
to love each other by a power unknown.
So remember this,
every time we kiss,
        My tongue inside your mouth, and over your
lips,
        Is like fire and desire running down our hips.
No one can change a thing but us.
It is me you know you can trust.
Keep in mind and all you do.
I am the ONLY woman for you!

For Love of Thyself

This magic moment, so into you
That I could not see anything else.
All the time I was searching to
Cure this lonely feeling from deep
Inside was just around the corner
Of my eyes.
You see, I live within a sudden emotion
That directs me to a place where no
Other can find.
A place where only I will ever be a
Part of.
A place that some type of mystery will
Occur at any given moment.
This place is called thyself!
For the love of you, there is no need
For loneliness.
For the love of you, I will find a point
Of uncertainty that no other can see.
For the love of thyself, only the magic
That leads to a dark hidden emotion
        Of romance that will always be entertaining
To the soul and the body at the same time
Will happen.
Oh yes for the love of thyself only you
And you alone will ever experience
How much joy it can be.
No matter what, there is no love unless
You can love thyself first.
And it all will fall into place.

The Makings of this Blackness

Juicy and so delicious is how I am built.
 I look at myself everyday when
I am blessed to wake up.
 Suddenly I kiss the air, because
I know where it will lead.
 As I follow the luxurious point
Of my toes out the door, I put my shades
 On and lock up.
Then as I walk down the street with my
 Head up, never looking down I see
Many turn at my big and tight buttocks.
 You see I know what I'm all
About. The blackness that I have been
 Blessed to hold up high is so
Real and unique, that even I am amazed
 At all that is.
I sense many wanting to know what my
 Secret is. There is none!
I love myself. Not because of the slight
 Almond shape eyes I have.
That is always carried with a sense of
 Awareness.
Not because of my big and lovely breast
 That seems to hold attention at the right
Time!
 Not that magnificent ass that get a glimpse
From many, wanting to just grab hold to it.
 And definitely not my thighs that carries
All of the above so well and stacked that I
 May look like a buxom princess.
It is just I. The Makings of this Blackness!

Cheek to Cheek!

I was dancing the other night in my
Bedroom, then the music stopped and I
Gazed up to the earth with my eyes
Closed and said, "Wow how sweet that was"
I could not digest at the time what was going
Through my mind because I thought it all was
A dream, however little did I know
There was a wind of whisper coming from behind
And as it held me tight, I grabbed on to
Myself and just took a deep breath. I could
Smell this type of aroma that no one else
Could have been wearing. Then I said is that
You? Without another word I looked
Into the darkness that suddenly disappeared
Because my eyes began to tear up just a bit.
I reached for the air and felt a warm touch
Down my back.
I said you did not leave me, so please don't.
Then as I smiled and grinned at the same
Time, this strong husk of air fell down on my
Cheek and stayed a while.
I felt so secure, and so less emotionally
Unattached that I left my face side
Ways with the attraction of this type of force.
Then finally as the lights began to shine
Once again and I could see the forest open
Up the doors of this type of magic
That occurred, I finally realized where and what
Should be. I realized that God was always in my corners of
darkness, you see, a light blew out of my soul. Then, God took his
own personal power and let me dance with him
Cheek to Cheek!

A Real Black Woman

It took 74 years to finally be
    Recognized!
Not because we did not deserve it.
    Or earn it!
Many women have come and gone.
When we sat there, not even
    Anticipating.
She sang her way to the top
With a lot of class.
Notice and unnoticed at the
Same time, but even she was patient!
Then came another strong one
In her part as a fighter.
Do you think they would talk
About all that she went through during
    Those tragic moments?
Why is it that we as Black women
Always get the short end of the
    Stick?
Well, if you really think about it,
    We are the long ends!
We are the backbones to your spine
We are the legs you stand on!
We are the birth and after birth of your
    Souls!
We have been formed and built to fit
    everyone's needs.
So, it does not matter if we are
Noticed or recognized by any
Of you, know that we are more than
Just a seed waiting to be developed.
We are Real Black Women!

So Fresh and So Clean

At 18 I decided to make a change in
Myself. It was time to open up the doors
To a little wonder.
I made this conscious decision to find my
Way home.
So, I got up one morning and said that
I was going to walk down the aisle and
Become a member.
It had been just about 5 years since I was a
Part of the congregation.
Then after uniting with all of them as a
Whole, 3 Sundays later I said
I want to be much more renewed!
So I went in the back where they helped
Dressed me as I put on all white.
My son who was 4 at the time had black
On.
As I walk back within the congregation
I sat with others who also decided to
Become anew.
I looked up at my heavenly father and said
Well this is it!
As I approached the steps and walked
Down in the water I was place carefully
In from my back over my face.
I have bath every night whether it is in the
Shower or bath tub but, this was a bath
Like no other.
I was clean! So Fresh and clean that there
Is no kind of dirt that can come onto this
Body: I have been baptized!

Part Six Of This Journey!

Spoken like a trooper throughout these past parts. I love LOVE don't you? So, as we step back into the real world of sensuous, let me say this: Being romantic is a given for some, but we have to determine what the definition of romance is. Tell me something!

Is it always about sugar and candy? Or maybe a slice of cake or pie? What is romance? Some of you need a lesson or two. I am inviting all of you into this piece of my world. The world at which I reside in, where I have experience what I determine to be some of the most romantic things you can do with your partner. The love that trembles down our souls is so magnifying to the eye that we must determine how to reach for the height of it. Can you do that?

I think personally for me and my significant other is the most romantic

And sexy couple out there. But I am bias because I know how to love. How about you? Share my world in a sense of fashion and take a little advice from this piece of me. I am never afraid to share what I have with you, because that is what this is all about! Love and sharing it to the world.

<u>Dancing and Romancing is More than An Undertone!</u>

The night is young. Music strolls down memory lane, but you are walking alone.

Silent night, but holy is what it is. As I watched your hora becoming much clearer to the eye, I wet my lips a bit. Can I just taste all that there is to offer of you?

Meek and humble as you stand, but I See right through it all. You want me more than ever!

I know this because the sweat that pours down your veins of attention stands mighty still when I am around.

I'm not gonna say, "is that a pistle in your pocket? I know what holds the key to my magic under world.

Then, I came up behind you to whisper this point Of no return in your ear. "I'll make you an offer" I know you can't Refuse.

Suddenly as I looked back at those deep dark Eyes that are on you smooth face, I see a smile appear.

I want you! Like I have never wanted someone Before. Let me lick the wombs surrounding your pressure!

I will be the chocolate that you send me. But, Instead I would rather wrap myself up and enjoy you as you Pull the strings apart!

Suddenly as I knelt down to watch you lift me up again, there was a sharp memory dispatch.

And guess what?

For Our Life

For our life we have to follow
Extraordinary things.
For our life there will be many
Songs to sing.
For our life we live in a small
World of our own everyday.
For our life there's always some
Price to pay.
       For our life we sit in the palm of your hands
Shedding thoughts of love in many bands.
As we go forward with our life
       Someone or thing will appear close and far.
We should know where to direct our steps
Leading to another phase not a bar.
But for our life we must give thanks.
To all involved they hold many ranks.

A Birthday Suit Fit for a Queen!

	There is no way to describe what I see in
you!	So very tall and as handsome as ever!
Ooh!	Look at those lips! So very and peachy.
Umm!	I can't wait for you to walk. That ass.
Wow!	It has a stick to it that looks like I could
Damn!	Your chest has muscles that tighten as I
Ahh!	The stomach that is so flat with dimples
Ssss!	I started from you head. Beautiful as
You are!	I kissed it. Then down your fine art of
The neck!	I licked it! With my lips still on you I
Sucked it!	That is your strong nipple.
Shit!	Down your stomach there was no stopping!
	When I looked at your navel I squinched
A bit!	It was so deep that I had no other choice

But to put my tongue in it!

Then, there it was! The black pubic turned
full blown into manhood hairs that was soft and sexy and
absolutely so sweet to the inviting eye.

I stared and watched you lay back with your
hands behind your head. As you looked down at me to say
"So what are you going to do next'? I could not help but find my
way home.

I massaged the oil of affection right through it
all. Then moisture just left my lips all over those soft hairs of love.
I looked up at you just enough for my eyes to stay glued to yours
as you wondered.

I am going to make you mines all day and the
rest of this night. I will be your queen and when I raise my body
on yours, this birthday suit you are wearing will be fit for me!

So I lift myself up and over with my thighs
Big and juicy (both of them) just around your face and watched
you love me absolutely just right! Happy Birthday!

117

That Dynamic Chemistry

From day one when we went out
I knew it was you!
You I connected with
You, I vibed with,
You were my soul mate
When we kissed, it felt as I was living
In you!
How is that? My womanhood felt joined
To your manhood
Then you stared at me, gleaming eye to eye
I had No idea, this is how you were
I found out, the secret passion
As you brought so much out
With me on the bottom, sometimes top,
Even on the side
And you, each and every where your black
Beautiful coin of love slipped into so wet!
I stood there and just stared at you!
You did the same!
We turned day into night very fast, like
It was the end of time!
Damn
I have never felt such Dynamic Chemistry
Like ours!
Kiss me now, and let my clothes fall off!

Don't Say Nothing, Just Whisper!

Many times we think when we lay in each other's arm, we need to discuss issues pertaining to our feelings for one another.

Right after you had soothe my over laid body with hot vibration of your kisses, was enough to make me quiver.

Don't misunderstand what I am saying.
Love in the right way is most sensational!

We need not say a word to the other because, our bodies spoke for themselves!

The heat of passion slipped in and out of my lips of affection, right down where it mattered most.

So don't say nothing, just whisper!
Whisper all the tinted airs of Jazz through the sexy crevices of my backbone.

Blow nice and nasty words all over my nipples as they hold up tight and high.

Whistle all of the above in one single puff of wisdom.   Don't say nothing, just whisper!
I need you to explore all the openings of THIS body of THIS universe that cries out loud and clear, so your mellow of mystifying Magic below the waist can hear it and attend to it gracefully.

Rise high up and gaze at my eyes as they water from tears of joy.

The oil continues to roll down your back as my tongue catches every drop I hum a song only your ears can hear.

So, please whatever you do, don't say nothing, just whisper!

Say it in any form or fashion you want, but,
Don't say nothing, just whisper!
Is it good? Hell yeah!
Can you feel it? What do you think?

Everything you do to me is like two birds in a cage of hopelessness going for the gold and winning!

Motivation-yes

All the more reason I want you!

Sensation- of course

Only you can fulfill

Admiration- a must

That's why I am with you.

Deliberations- has happened all the way

So take me up and out as I bring your face closer to my womanhood.

Don't say nothing, just whisper!

Then listen to what is said back, I Love You!

When We Join Together Climatically!

I tried to resist being around you, touching
      You and kissing you.
But, when you pulled me closer, I pushed
      Away a bit.
You said to me "Who is it?"
      Tell me!
I was turned on by your direct approach.
      You grabbed me with an erotic force,
And asked me again.
      I would not say.
Then you grazed my face with the tenderness
      Of your lips, so I gave in.
As our bodies washed up and down with the
      Love we shared, I grew much more
In tuned to the reality of my soul.
      It seemed no matter how I resisted, I
Could not! I wanted it! I needed it! I
      Had to have it! And all it was is you!
So I gravitated on all you came at me with
      And we join together, climatically!

The Mind of Misery

Stars in the sky is just a slight ways of
Some type of fantasy.
I fantasize about you all the time.
I have grown to take it to another level.
Feel what I am saying.
       Touch my erogenous zone layer of affection.
The mind of misery tries to get in the way.
It keeps taking me to a level that is not even
A part of this vocabulary that I carry with
Me in an everyday fashion.
The mind of misery is for people who
Have no life.
The mind of misery will keep all in denial.
The mind of misery takes all of us to a new
Phase of hatred.
It's all about love, or did you know that?
Love conquers all in everything we do!
The mind of misery never exist if we only
Stick to our human guns.
Place your hands over my heart.
It's ok to feel my breast, because they are
There.
But if there is peace within your mind
Misery can never enter!

If Ever I learned

If ever I learned to trust you as I did
      Before.
I would not have to hurt because of still
      Loving you some more.
If ever I learned that someone was true.
      There is no pain to come before you.
If ever I learned to don't give you my all.
      Time will pass and I'd have a ball.
If ever I learned to find myself to be real
      Nothing you could say can close
      Any deal.
But fear not at all I say, learning is never
      A price to pay.
The rewards stand perfect and still.
      Because if ever I learned was to
Climb up the highest hill.
      Always remember to take every lesson
In stride.
      There are no secrets ever to hide.
        If ever I learned that a man
would be a man,
      I won't take a chance by far if I can.
Faith is important in all that we do
      If ever I learned God taught me a few.

On The Shore

My soul was born to exceed any type
Of naked truth that turns into a lie.
          I walked down towards the south street
And stuck my feet in it.
          As the sand reached in between my toe,
I felt the salt curl up against my
Ankles.
          On the shore I closed my eyes and said
Thank you father, I have been reborn
To you all over.
I found true love.
Love of thy nature and thy self.
On the shore, there was man standing
Some what far and close at the same
Time.
All though it was night the sun
Still shined!
The man was looking at me straight
In the eyes but he was blind.
As he stood I walked closer and
Further from him to see what he
Really was like.
          The shore makes
many different things
Happen to us.

As I reached into the salt water,
I noticed that he was gone.
Then I walked over to the spot
That he stood and looked at the
Ground.
He left a small token for me to
Keep.
It was a halo,

Stay The Night

The morning breathe of sunshine just
    Takes everything out of me, but I feel
Alive and well. I kiss the air of
Acknowledgement just to see how close
My lips will touch the earth.
The moon was glowing through the wind
Right after the sun came up. Who
Would have thought?
I looked over my shoulder just to see
If the darkness that disappeared the
Other day would still haunt me just a bit.
As I glared into the mirror, a rage of light
Came down from the heart of this universe
And I bowed downed to all the success
Beneath every bit of the sunshine.
I kept thinking back on it all.
        I remembered those sudden
dreams that came
About last night and I smiled with
all my pearly white teeth so happy.
I saw you stare at me as I was sleeping.
No I did not imagine it, you were there!
I moved closer to the other side of the bed
Felt a little hint of affection but I did not
        Get beside myself, I just
continued to sleep.
        Some time in the middle of the
night I had to
Turn over and move down just a bit, and
When I opened my eyes I saw you.
You were not right up on me, but very near.
You made me feel whole! I began to grab

Hold to both my arms and cling tighter.
At that very moment, a strong breeze came
About through my hair. I took a deep sigh
Of relief and said, "I know you are always
With me father" I know I am resting
Peacefully tonight because you sang me
A song. You rocked me like a baby with
The sweetest story that I have ever heard.
I know my dreams have come to a reality
Because you made it happen so, I fear not
If my soul is still here to stay, it is you
That will comfort me. And my body?
Well, I came onto this earth in the form
Of a woman. As the dust appears turned
My skin to the other side of magic.
So, my heavenly father, Stay the Night!

Mocha Chocolate

I don't care what color you may choose
To insert into you vaginal facilitated area,
But, I choose Mocha chocolate.
Do you want to know why?
I love sweets! The taste just drives me
Absolutely crazy. Do you know what it is
       To have mocha chocolate enter
you wombs of
       Affection. It's so good and so
delectable that
I can't imagine anything else.
Don't get me wrong, white chocolate is ok
If it has the right amount of sugar, but
That wonderful flavor of mocha is the best.
It's just not enough of it around.
Everyday becomes harder and harder.
You see, once you get hip to the flavor,
       Oh boy! What have you gotten
yourself into.
If only some of these others kinds keep up
       With there own kind. Then maybe
we would
Not have to share our Mocha Chocolate!

A Kept Woman

It's easy to say to a woman how
Much you love her and want to
Spend a lot of time with her,
But, when there is another woman
What do you do?
I mean, if you want to be shared
There are a certain amount of rules
That must be followed.
Let me see: Well #1 is about
Sacrifice. How much is the woman
That is sharing you sacrificing to stay
                    In the relationship,
therefore you have
To make up with her what she is not
Fully getting from you.
#2: Some bills need to be met!
After all, if you are living with some
One else, then why should she have to
Suffer and pay her own bills if the
                    Other woman is not.
And, ain't nothing
Going on but the rent!
#3: sex- I mean even if it is good, why
are you using her place instead of a
hotel. Give her what you would pay
for a hotel/motel, nothing is free.
#4 Leave her some money at the
end of your visit or the beginning

if you are worth some of her chime
why not give her a little something
to show her you care. Flowers will
not always do!
There are certain things that must
Be followed if you want a Kept
Woman! On the other hand,
What woman wants to BE kept by
A man like you?

<u>Within the Heart Minus the Aggravation!</u>

We learn everyday about sharing ourselves with one another.

Loving, caring, and being sympathetic to each others need.

Sometimes we give a little too much, and sometimes not enough.

But, when you decide to be totally true to the cause, it turns soar.

Whether it is family, friends or even a loved one, there is no need for aggravation!

I think people who get inside your head or heart decides the many issues pertaining to everything but what they really should.

Of course you know that we don't have to deal with any of this B--- S---!

What I am saying is this: we give so much of us to those who don't know what to do with it.

It's all within the heart, but minus the aggravation, works well as far as I'm concern, because frankly, I don't need the shit!

I'd rather stick with myself!

<u>*Your Hands*</u>

I not only get the gentle caressing of your touch with them, and it's not the hard core lines I see across the, showing your work force.

Not even the way you lift up heavy things as you do. But, the strength I see as I wave them around, sticks in my heart. How you grab hold tight onto something large.

Your hands are most sensual as you run your fingers up my back.

Your hands are very strong the way you force different instruments into place.

Your hands are most tantalizing as I lick every tip on the fingers while gazing in your eyes.

Your hands when holding mines makes me feel secure with you. Knowing you are leading the way.

I adore every bit of your body, but your hands make all the difference when we are together!

Your Love of Music Makes all The Difference

The day after the nigh we met,
you made me
Two tapes.
You knew I loved music so you responded.
As our love grew stronger, your music
Increased.
But the lyrics became most intense.
We had some hard times and good times!
Then the music decreased.
I loved you so much but I couldn't see
How you felt.
The way you expressed it was different
from me.
Then one day, you gave me a tape that
said it all.
When you presented it to me, I really didn't
listen to it, but I decided to listen to it.
As I sat at my desk and analyzed every
song of your choice, every word.
The tears rolled down my face.
For the love I give you, Somebody loves
you Girl, Cause I love you, the touch of
You, You and I, Oh Girl.
These songs spoke for you.
Your love of this kind of music makes all
the difference to me. You don't have to
say anything, I just have to listen to the
music you give to me, because it expresses
what you feel.
Thank you for showing me how special you
express love this way.

What You Do to Me

Bent on being angry. Trying to force a hold
    From within.
I can't stand to look at you! My mind keeps
Circulating all around the past and every little
Thing you said and done.
I could not even look at you. Not because you
Aren't gorgeous, but I know if I do I will fall
Again. Your smile and eyes is what took me the
Very first time.
So, every moment I get I try to turn it off.
Turn off the fact that you have such
Moisturizing lips of sanction easy to kiss.
Turn away from your stunning boyish face
That makes you look 10 years younger.
Not get hypnotize by those EYES, I get glued to
Every time you stare at me.
Think about what lies between your legs.
God knows I have never seen so many inches.
And your gentle touch when you lay me down
Then pull me closer to you.
When we rolled together your scent is like a
Melody I have tilted in my dreams. I lay
My nose over the hair cut that fits your face
So perfect. The oil you massage in it draws
Me nearer to your thrown.
Oh, what you do to me, I can't explain.
All I know is this, no matter what, no other will
And can take your place. You are someone so
Different than I have ever known.
You make me want you more and more, then
After I see you I smile. I can't be mad!

The Test of Time

Leaving you was a big mistake!
With all I was missing caused
More of a heartache!
Your form, your warmth, your tender
        Touch!
Oh how I really, really, wished for
        Your touch.
But time is known to heal all scars!
Doesn't matter how man, there's
One that stands stranger than bars!
What I knew was more than you will
        Ever feel.
Once upon a time I felt my love was
        Real.
Although, now the test of time will
        Tell all!
I see a different light shining above
        The hall.
I panic; I sweat, just to see your smile
Because I know, when I hold you
        It's worth the while!
The test itself was meant for me!
To show that time away from you
        Will be.
Just know I've waited this long for
        You,
Quality stands only for a few.
The test of time is my heart!
That beats stronger when you come
Back, my love will last longer.

    I Love You!

I Can't Answer Why?

God walks with me through every situation.
    When times are rough
    When times are good.
I can't answer why it goes this way.
I can't answer why I decide another.
    Just as I began to think my skin
        Had turned rough,
through all the silliness that I encounter.
    I tossed and turn for answer from
        Within.
But I never get them at the time.
    Then suddenly the wool has lift up
        and over.
Leaving me lost and baffled along the
        hidden road.
I can't answer why? I can't tell you how?
        I am trying as hard as I could.
Many others have slipped away. As I
        looked to the heavens to search
for the answer, it all disappeared!
    I can't answer why? I felt your
Spirit in my soul mixing up a brand new
        Emotion.
I can't answer why? I have not put all
    my trust into us again.
All I know is when I love you over and
    over again, it feels right.
God opens the door through my heart
    For me to love you, and you to love
        me.
I can't answer why? Cause I don't know

A Love Jones All over Again!

One week after I said things that hurt, I dug deep down inside of myself and pulled out every bit of anger that held me down.

You appeared before my eyes although you were not physically there-

I still love you- no matter what! I thought I did the right thing by telling you to leave-

I thought what I said would stick inside my gut, because I thought I was right and you were wrong-

I could not believe you would walk away and not turn back-

But, a few days later not even a week, I glanced back at it all and just cried.

I cried, because you were not there anymore.

I cried, because I was the one hurting from my own words.

I cried, because I missed you so much and you did not listen to my hurt.

I just cried at all of it.

But, no one understands what I feel!

They think that I am stupid for loving you so much!

They think I should move on-but, this goes deeper than the average Love Jones.

My heart is in it so deeply. Our love goes way above any cloud, and way inside the souls of a Valentines Day holiday.

We know what it's all about!

And who cares if no one else does.

We will move forward at the pace that God put before us as he leads the way.

This is more than a Love Jones all over ag

That Handsome Look of Your Soothing Awakening

As you lied there next to me holding
Your arms around me ever so tight,
I looked up to see that oh so beautiful
Smile from those ever so tantalizing
      Lips on your face.
I felt secure. I felt whole. I felt your
      Love.
Then you lifted that blackness of your
Chest just above where I had to look
      Up.
I stared without a blink! Because you
      Are so handsome!
You kissed me and I melt.
I could not help but allow the tears to
Continue to fall down my cheekbones.
I laid back thinking about the day we
First met. How I thought you were
Too young, and where we are today.
As you kept looking at my face, my
Hair, my body, I decided to let you
      Just have me.
I think that you are just wonderful!
The way you hold my chin and suck
On my tongue, my lips, my mouth,
My breast, I close my eyes to forgive
All the many mistakes we made along
      The way.
Your handsome face soothes my ever
Lasting trace of any non glory of the
Past to return me to the present.
So here me now to all that I have to

Say,
As the many possibilities that life
Stands to offer us as a whole,
You are the one, who has filled my
     Love soul!
If anyone else thought they had
     A chance.
It would not be me to save them the
     Last dance.
It is you! With all the love on that
     Wonderful face.
That I know personally, no other
     Man can ever trace.
It is not just the way you hold me tight.
But it's how you can make love to me
     All night!
So listen clear to all I have said,
I adore you all over and under not
Just what you can do in the bed!

Chocolate Romance

As the night grew long,
The Dee Jay continued to play
        Another song.
Then you asked me to dance,
At that time I said I'd take a chance.
I noticed your body formed and
                Fit!
Made me raise my eyebrows and
        Say, "Damn, he's the shit"!
        Then I swayed my body all
                Around,
Feeling the music, getting into
        The sound.
You said "don't mind me while I
        Watch the show"
I smiled and thought, girl this is
        The way to go!
But still in all I was just having
        Fun.
Not thinking about anything or
        Even ready to run.
Then you said, "Can I buy you a
        Drink?
I looked and thought, huh, what
        Do you think?
As we talked for a little while,
I said to myself this number he will
        Never dial.
Low and behold what happened after
        That night,
We started dating becoming hardly
        Out of each other's sight.

All I can say is that night was a
Surprise!
Never thought that this man would
Capture my eyes!
But as days go on and nights too
I miss every moment that
I can't see you!
One thing I know for sure was
That dance,
Turned into a chocolate
Romance!

We are so sweet together!

The Confession

Two years ago I went through the ultimate love revelation the night
after she found out. I decided not to say a word until the other day.

I never thought it would come to me to
tell you all that I see.

I said, you want to hear my confession?
You just listened.

One night after that altercation we had two years
ago, I missed you so!

As I always do, I lit a candle for you!

Then I turned to God and asked for his
word.

I did not know what was in store for
our future after what happened and all I heard.

I smelt your scent upon my pillow, but
all I could do was cry like a weeping willow!

I wanted you bad just to be near me.
Your face and smile was all I could see!

So the next best thing that I could do,
Was put your shirt by my side and think it was you.

I confess my love was very strong,
I did not want to hurt anyone because I know it would be wrong!

But as time went on to many other days,
I realize what happen was not just a phase.

Now, and then, my love was real,
We have gone through so much I know it's time for my heart to heal.

In the meantime as we move on, I pray
that God forgives me if I should have just moved along.

I can't say if we will ever end, but this
is my confession to you who is more than a friend!

Every Whim of Your Touch

Just a little bit is all it takes!
The finger tips of your soul,
To my skin makes me curl.
I don't know what it is, except
I'm so crazy about you!
You have kissed my lips more
Than a thousand times but, it
Always seems like the first.
When we see each other, my eyes,
Your eyes, are so mesmerizing, that
We capture the glow over and over
            Again!
When you kiss my hands, my feet,
My stomach, Oh what a treat!
You are the man!
The one and only who fills me,
And discover my reflections all
Over again!
I really don't mind if you stare,
I know you can't help it.
The magnetism of our thoughts
Draw us closer together.
I asked you one day, why can't we be
            Apart?
You said, "We love each other"
Every whim of your touch
Means so much!
Those hands on my legs and thighs
Make me oh so high!
Sweet mouth and lips always ready to
            Kiss,
Don't leave me now, cause you will

Be missed.
Let me share myself with you.
                    There are so many
things that we can do.
Every whim of your touch,
Is like fire and desire between my legs
Ready for you to clutch.
                    And once more. We
start all over again,
Because every whim of your touch
Makes me write more of my love.
To you I send!
What we have together, let no man or
Woman takes it apart!

How Special You Are

About 5 years ago I saw you as a
One of a kind party friend.
Then before I knew it, something
Happened!
We were drawn to each other like a
Magnifying glass of this sort of
Attentiveness.
Every since then, I have
been feeling my
Way through your Soul!
How special are you in my heart?
Let me tell you. I observed your
solid hands
Hold things tight with such a strong
Grip, (the way you hold
My buttocks) when we embrace each other.
Your work ethics really turn me on,
As you take careful consideration of all
Your surroundings, (that's
how gentle
You are when we kiss).
I though once we turned our
friendship
Into a romance, things would change.
I found out that our bodies of Spirit
United a long time ago!
There is a place within my heart that
Holds someone special that is you!
I see and feel your pain. I feel and
See your pleasure. I smell and see your
Desire to want more from.
us, but don't

145

Give up! I am opened to enter your heart.
It may have taken some tosses and
            Turns to get there, and even at
times it seemed
            I was giving up.
Then there were moments you stood me up
Because of your own insecurities.
            I looked over it all because I knew
How special you are in my heart.
            I adore you more than you know!
And I want us to reach that point beyond
            The erection that protrudes when you
Walk in my office towards me.
            I want us to count the many stars
And rainbow shines that will light up when
            We look at each other.
You see, I am more than just a woman!
            I am your destiny and you are my
                        Future!

Part Seven Of This Journey!

What is the definition of friends? I have the faintest ideas in my head but how I defined it is my way of expressing the love in all.

There are no former rules to loving a friend or just seeing someone close to you when needed. I have experienced joy and pain when it came to individuals I identified as a friend. I had to search very carefully within my soul and heart to get all the answers.
Today I still am looking for answers to my questions for who is and who is not what they call a friend.

Unfortunately like many, I have succumbed to bad breaks with people misleading the way. I have learned through the power of my mother/father God, on what is the best direction for me to follow in all that I do, and in all I see in people.

This section is devoted and dedicated to the many friends in my life who have shown me their courage of no destruction. In this I mean truth within all. They were there for me at many occasions that I did not expect. But I know they came for a reason. God's reason!

So let me take the time to let all of you listen to what I have learned from these people who came into my life throughout this journey I go along with called Life!
This is dedicated to all of them!

A Deep Secret

One of the best people I could have
    Known
    He carried a great sense of compassion
    That everyone could love.
A not so maybe family man.
    When I first laid my eyes on
Him, I thought he was really a good
    Looking guy.
I learned this very first time that you
    Can fall in love with a person
Just to be a friend.
    He and I are so in touch with
Ones own feelings that we are there
               For one another
more than ever.
There is so much to be found when
    You find a man or a woman
That you can share it all with, when
    There is no sex involved.
I admire you whole hearted for
    Just being my friend!
Let me say this to you:
When we speak I am never blue.
              You have given the
meaning of friends

A whole new name.
                    No matter what
anyone say it is not the
Same.
The closeness I feel is more than you
Know.
I recognize the many things you do for
me is a nice way to go.
Thank you for being my friend and
More. Not just a big secret like before.

I have a Different Love for you!

Over 4 years ago I admired the way
You worked with me.
One of the many people who was
                    Most conscious about
getting the work
Done.
I liked that.
You always teased me a bit.
Never figured you to be my type.
A ladies man and all.
I would see you in the clubs really
Living it up!
But I had eyes for your friend.
And all we were was friends.
You never gave me the impression
That you wanted me.
I just did not see you that way.
Low and behold there was a key of
Magic even I could not see.
We decided to move to another
Level. It was passionate for the
Time period we provided.
But today, things are different
Oh yea, don't mistake what I am
Saying, I still love you! In my own
Way. I have a different love for you.
A love that has changed to a strong
Friendship, I am sure you will always
Be the person that God made you.
Thank you for all the respect and love
Back that has been a part of us.
And thank you for just being you

A Window Through my Heart

I have found true life with willingness.
    You are my friend!
Every since yesterday over two
    Decades ago I met you.
Very funny and free.
    I always thought very high
Of you.
    Just as pretty as can be.
A family you came from with such a
        Bond.
You took me in as a sister the day we
    First met.
I could say anything to you and trust
    It would not go any further.
I never said much about this:
    But what I want you to know
Leslie is, I Love you Girl.
    I wish we were in touch more!
But no matter how long it is that we
    Are apart, I will always
Remember and trust all the friendship
    We shared and put it in my
Own bank of treasure chest knowing
    Until this day no other person
Has had a window through my heart
    As you do.
        You never judged me,
and I thank you
    For that.
        You have always been
honest with me.
        And never

brought any unwanted
Advice to my door.
   If there ever was a time I needed
A friend, you were there.
   Now it's time for me to give
Back to you.
   Leslie Beatty Johnson.
I want to let you know, this ones
   For you!
Peace will stay within our friendship
   From now until on.
Thank you my friend, for keeping
   These windows in my heart
      Clean!

We May Not Approve of Some Our Others, But it's Ok

Spirit is alive and well within the five of us.
 After voicing and being whom we
are in this
Group has come to many calls.
We have demonstrated trust and love to
No return.
We may not approve of some of our others
But it's ok.
We all have other friends.
We have family.
But it's just so sweet the bond that the
Five of us have formed that makes our
Soul unbreakable.
It does not matter how many Barbara's
Come around.
There is a special Barbara with us, who in
God inserted fact.
The original Sisters of the Light with the
Name of heavens hold.
We are truth of amazement!
We're gonna be there with this extra power
From the Holy Spirit, that kept us alive
As we are.
We may not approve of some of our others
But it's ok!
We're staying strong and learning from the
Other that What God joins together, let
NO man or woman, tears it apart!

Part Eight Of This Journey!

This section is dedicated to the little ones in our lives that we have been blessed to bore. Me, being a mother of three beautiful children is most joyful! I am allowing all of you to take a peak into my children's talent with lots of love behind it.

Dana and Kenneth, share their joy with you, so take a look at these two young people, and what they have to say from their soul and experience another wonderful part of this universe of theirs and ours. From the love of our children to the one they love.

Peace within is what this is all about!

Light Skin

Dana Parker

I'm a pretty young lady
Who's light skin and proud of it!
Light skin Isn't White!
I am a light skin strong beautiful girl.
That's who I am!
You don't have to be dark to have a pretty
        Smile,
Or even dress decently.
           You can be white, orange, or any other color
To be in a video.
My mother brought me out into this
world and taught me to stand up for who I am!
And represent myself well.
Not what someone judge me by.
I am a future lawyer who will stand up
For what's right and wrong.
I don't know who you are? But, I know
I'm a beautiful light skin young lady
Who has a lot of courage in herself?
That is who I am and will always be!

Children

Being young not knowing any better.
    I thought all I did was a
    Breeze like the whether.
I mesmerized about having a family
    With 2 kids.
While playing with clay covering all
    The lids.
When I grew up, things were not the
      Same.
I had a lot to do no time for that
      Game.
Being a child is some fun.
    Being an adult there is nowhere
To run.
    I have children of my own now.
Sometimes I don't know what to do
    And how.
But children are so great to the mother of,
      It's like a smooth swan or
even a dove.
I can't turn what I did as a child back,
    I will love the memories and run
On another track.
    No matter what, if you are around
Children, enjoy all the time to care.
    Don't make them feel silly or
Or act like they are hard to bare.
    These little ones are our future
That life will hold.
    Never any what may become of them
I'm sure some can be very bold
But it's ok in the long run, Trust me!

<u>All of My Love to You</u>

Everyday I wake up to see how beautiful
       You are.
The love I feel inside me is so strong. I
       Would never have imagined this.
As soon as I opened my eyes, I think
       About going to your rooms
And watch you sleep.
       Such a lovely face both you have,
So peaceful, so tender.
       There is so much joy in your closing
Eyes.
       I admire both of you!
Not because of the precious hands God
       Placed before me, to hold you.
Not because you are so smart!
Not because you remind me of myself!
       Just because, you are this
wonderful creature
       I had the honor of giving birth to.
For all of my love to you is what a
       Mother should always explore
       And apply!

For Dana and Kenneth

Hard Work   By Dana Parker

From Kindergarten until the eighth grade,
I worked hard doing what I did to be able
To get to High School.
I am not there yet, but soon I will be.
Grades 7 and 8th I really did not have
       Great expectations,
But, as I studied and paid more attention
I continued to hand in my homework
But I call it hard work!
I may not have over a 90 average, and I
May not be perfect, but at least I am on
       The right track to being the best that I can be!
Every tear I dropped when it came to The
       Parent Teachers Conferences, would not help
With my work.
Only my brain and much more confidence,
Would do me hard work in my life!

Black People

Black People understand their color.
Black people some time tell lies on their
Own.
But never apologize for what they say.
Black people know many things.
Black people are called African Americans.
But when the bell rings in their
many chiming
Days.
Black people finally feel very good in all
Ways.
Blacks are very hard workers.
So that makes me happy and I say hooray!

Kenneth Blassingame

Love Wishes and A Thin Line
Between Love and Hate

Love wishes are love thoughts.
Even though you don't love someone
But you love God.

Always when you wish,
You enjoy yourself.

My journey is a beginner
Journey of wishes.

If you think wrong,
Then don't think at all!

Thin line between love and hate
Is a strong feeling.

If you love someone nice and smooth,
Then it's right!

But, if you love someone that is mean
And loves you at the same time,
Then it is a Thin Line Between Love
          And Hate!

Kenneth K Blassingame

The Finale!

As I close this book by saying no matter what, love will conquer everything. We must learn to love each other and stop all the ugly surroundings that make us HATE. Oh yea, I have made plenty of mistakes, myself, but when I find that something is just not working for the benefit of me and whoever involved, I sit back and reflect back on what really is going on.

We are a oneness no matter what! God has blessed us with the realization of finding how to gain the happiness we deserve. There is not a single person that should NOT have love in their lives. I write about love, peace, and harmony because I know it can happen.

Not just for me, not just for you, but also for everyone. We start strong at first, and then the weakness comes about. Instead of us knocking it back to the door it came from, we take it in and use it against others.

As you can see, many of the poems I wrote about love, were not just about the actual part of being in love but, the experience behind it, whether it turns into something we did not expect or if it involves another person or within our own children. The one thing about life is we all experience the same things as the other, so I am sure there is a poem in this book that we all can relate to.

This is Dedicated to the One's I love is more than from me to you.

It's about the power to express you! The reasons behind why I even loved, love, or is still loving you? The motion of knowing how to feel. The emotional, physical, and mental challenge we face in relationships.

It's from me to you, my lover, brother, mother, sister, or whoever.

I want to take this time to say to all of you, I dedicate this book to you! Peace and Blessings to the world! May we shine among each other, with the everlasting patience from the Spirit within. Let us be guided by the force of no turning back and the point of divine emotion. Just remember, don' take it personal what I write. It's all about growth and understanding how to make it better. We are all still a oneness and sisters and brothers of love. No matter what, when it comes down to it, we are all his children.

The Epilogue!

Poetry comes from the many different parts of our lives that we share whether it be with someone we know or alone. When we go to work, that is poetry! When we wake up in the morning that is poetry! When we encounter another part of our life we never knew existed that is poetry! Oh how awesome it feels to see a light through the honor of knowing poetry. As I walk through the valley of knowing it and experiencing it every part of this day as well as any day, it puts a smile on my face to be able to put my words in the form of understanding what may be going on in my life. I am happy to share the many experiences I have encountered with all of you.

Love in our lives is most wonderful to be a part of. There is no mountain high enough for me to climb to get to the destination where I am appointed to be. With the Love of God behind me is what keeps me willing and able to carry any burdens that may turn to a blessing to the final phase of this journey I have walked through many years ago, called "life".

His love and my love of him has been the best part of living. The gift I have been blessed with of writing to all of you out there have made my wonderful way of living not only a challenge to look forward to on a daily base but a miracle itself. Happy is what it will be! You make it happy for yourself in any way necessary to move forward. Do it for yourself and not for another.

Keep all in life as a blessing and remember experience is another learning part of blessings, nothing good comes easy. For the most part, be kind to one another!

This is dedicated to all of you, within every peaceful part in my heart; I am and will always be,
"inspiration"

This is Dedicated to the One I Love

In life experience's we have ups and downs,

Peace and happiness is just around the corner.

My life with you has been so moving; I can't explain what you do to me!

I know that love is standing before me, and your arms are opened wide.

How you embraced me makes me whole,

You loving me makes me who I am!

It is you God that I love the most!

All that I am, and all that I can be, is the mark of all I believe!

If I had to do it all over again, I would not hesitate!

This is for you, and all that you are!

God, This is dedicated to you, the one I Truly Love!

Waking Up to Glory

What a wonderful year this has been
    Waking up to the Glory!
If it was not for you, I could not have
        Don't it!
What?   Live?   Be who I am?

There's no perfect one than you Lord!
    And as I continue on this
    Journey called "Life"

I am waking up to the Glory!
 The Glory of you!
The Glory of Love!
The Glory of Hope!
The Glory of all possibilities!
Yes, you made me to feel this way,
And there is NO secret to this Supernatural
        Journey!
Just, waking up to the Glory, Your Glory
    Father God!

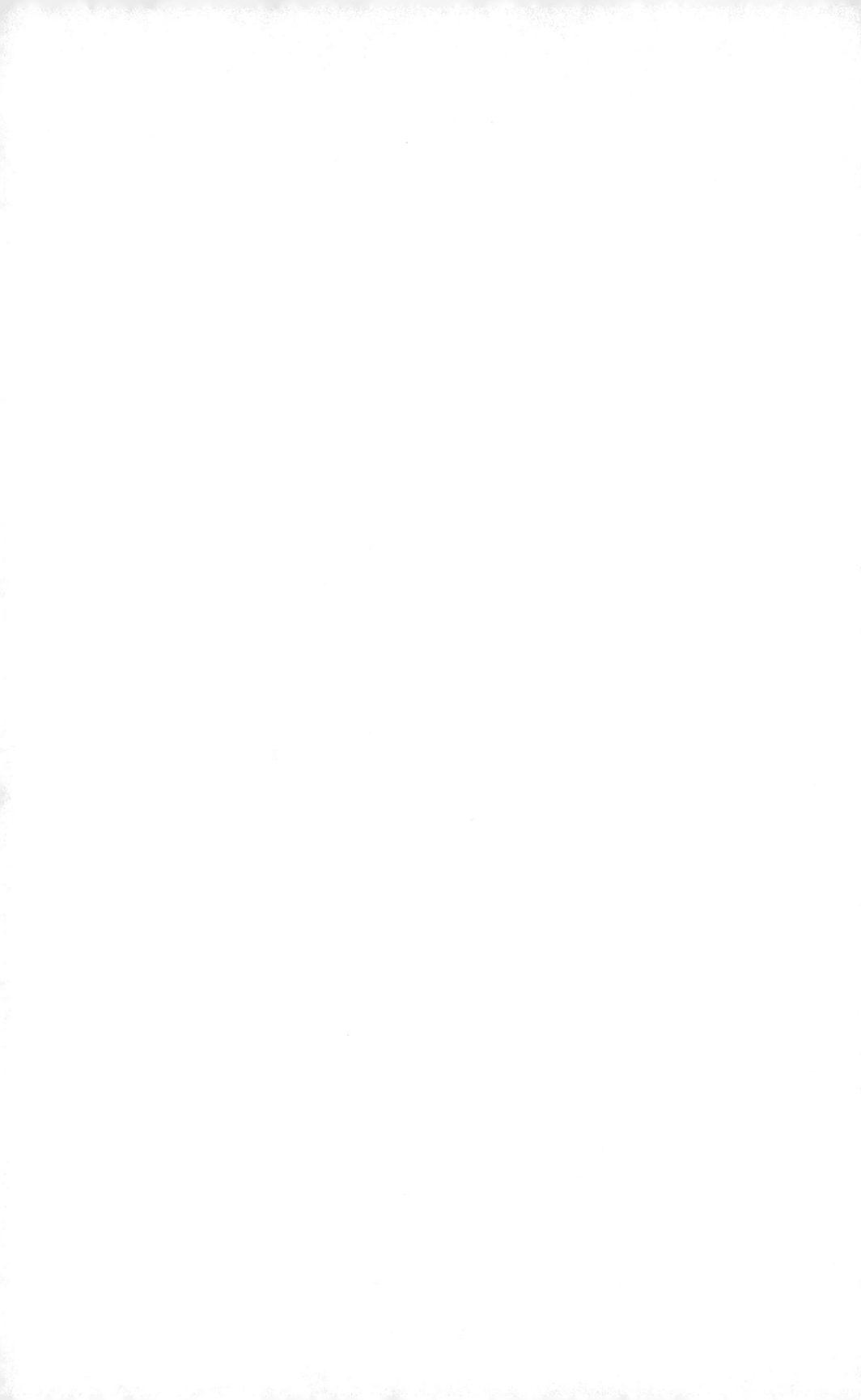

www.ingramcontent.com/pod-product-compliance
Lightning Source LLC
Chambersburg PA
CBHW030944180526
45163CB00002B/695